Unflappable

6 Steps to Staying
Happy, Centered, and Peaceful
No Matter What

Ragini Elizabeth Michaels

MJF BOOKS
NEW YORK

Published by MJF Books
Fine Communications
322 Eighth Avenue
New York, NY 10001

Unflappable
LC Control Number: 2015959280
ISBN 978-1-60671-342-6

Printed in the United States of America.

MJF Books and the MJF colophon are trademarks of Fine Creative Media, Inc.

QF   10   9   8   7   6   5   4   3   2   1

This work is dedicated to the power of our hearts and the insistent urge to love—over and above all things. And to those who hear this call and allow its ever-present pull to shape and guide their lives.

CONTENTS

PART TWO
YOUR MAP TO THE LAND OF UNRESOLVABLE DILEMMA AND THAT DIFFERENT BRAND OF HAPPINESS

ACKNOWLEDGMENTS

This book would never have been written without the generosity and kindness of so many friends, family, and colleagues. Here are just a few: Rick and Nadine Shanti, who gave me shelter, love, and support as I struggled to stay present and write from my heart; my oh-so-patient editors at Conari Press, Caroline Pincus, who saw the value in this work and championed it to completion, and Susie Pitzen, who somehow got me all the changes I asked for; Sondra Kornblatt, my writing mentor, whose humor, encouragement, and faith in me and the work kept me laughing through the pain and agony of crafting the perfect sentence; Ambodha and Rhonda Sable, who took care of my dog, Hafiz, when I couldn't take him with me and he had nowhere else to go; Renee Giovarelli and Gary Olmeim, tenaciously dedicated to personal transformation, and willing to share their awakenings along the way; Narayana Granatelli, Valerie Loebs, my sisters, Sue and Mary, and my brother, Ben, all tirelessly gave me encouragement, feedback, love, and acceptance; and all the students and clients who helped me uncover this wisdom by demonstrating their own courage, commitment, and faith in something larger than themselves. And finally, to Osho, and the legion of mystics throughout time who continue to show us the possibility of embodying peace and love. I thank you one and all.

Dear Reader,

I hope you will accept the wisdom in this book as a gesture of love—from my heart to yours. This wisdom helped me find true self-acceptance, peace of mind, and a kind of happiness I never knew existed. In short—my life finally became workable.

As a counselor and behavioral change specialist, I focus on *how* to get a new behavior to happen—whether it's eating healthy, saving money, or being more aware. Radically new behaviors require a change in your brain. *Unflappable* offers this kind of brain-changing perspective. It clears the way to use your capacity for inner peace and a different brand of happiness. Here are some of the ways you'll benefit:

- You'll become more content with where you are, moment to moment, instead of feeling there is someplace else you'd rather be.

- You'll relax and embrace continual change, instead of trying to control and manipulate life.

- You'll know you are on a journey of becoming more aware, moment to moment, instead of comparing yourself to people you believe are enlightened or better than you.

- You'll know how to embrace *both* the emotional roller-coaster ride of being human *and* the reflective calm of being divine, instead of being confused about where and how to fit spirituality into your daily life.

Unflappable provides insight, wisdom, and guidance so you can walk on a paradoxical path—a path that doesn't assume either your humanity or your divinity is better than the other, a path rich in practical possibilities for creating true happiness, in a better world.

May this wisdom help you find what you're seeking. Enjoy.

In peace and wonder,
Ragini

INTRODUCTION
THE CHASE AFTER HAPPINESS

"All I want is for you to be happy."

Did you ever hear your mother say that? Did you ever buy a house, take a trip, get a new job, or fall in love and think you had happiness in the bag—until reality and just plain life settled in?

"Happiness is there for the taking! Go get it!" That's what American culture tells us, with overwhelming evidence for its apparent truth all around: happy, rich, successful, beautiful folks on TV; well-dressed businesspeople bustling in and out of the glitzy high-rise buildings downtown; luxurious lifestyles portrayed in fashion magazines at the grocery store. Even though your pursuit might not sound so glamorous, this cultural decree defines how most people pursue happiness. But it doesn't give you the whole story about creating a happy life.

Here's the thing—the idea that you can catch happiness this way, and have it all the time, is like a mirage: it shimmers in the distance, beckoning you forward but is unable to ever deliver what it promises. Yet we cling to the idea of finding perpetual happiness as if it were a real oasis. We think we'll finally quench our persistent thirst to enjoy life and feel good.

The problem isn't that happiness isn't available to us right now—it's just not hiding out where we're looking.

> The idea that you can catch happiness this way, and have it all the time, is a mirage.

Is Happiness Even a Worthy Pursuit?

Everyone's searching for happiness in some way or another. But is it a worthwhile goal or just an indulgence? Should you be embarrassed at wanting it? Can you really be a good person if you focus on being happy? Or does wanting happiness for yourself mean that you're a selfish slacker, avoiding being a responsible, conscious and engaged global citizen?

The answer is a definite no! It's not only okay to be happy, but also it's your birthright—and your gift to share with others. The Dalai Lama says this is the purpose of our existence. Even the United States Declaration of Independence encourages your pursuit of happiness.

When I was four years old, I remember tiptoeing out of my room to the top of the staircase on Christmas morning. As I peeked down into the living room, my eyes landed on the most beautiful doll in the universe, unwrapped, waiting for me under the tree. I was so happy I shook with joy. That was my defining moment. I was convinced my purpose in life was to be happy. How could that not be? It felt *soooooooo* good. I never forgot that oh-so-excellent feeling. I wanted it again—and again, and again.

When I grew up, I realized that happiness does makes the heart overflow and lifts giving to a kingly stature—with so much in your heart, sharing is the only option. Like a cloud that has to rain to relieve the fullness of too much moisture, the human heart has to share happiness to relieve the fullness of too much joy.

What Works (and Doesn't) with Go-Get-It Happiness

I bet you've experienced that fullness of joy too. You may have felt it when you finally got your promotion, bought a house, finished that creative project you'd thought was beyond your reach, or saw your baby take those first steps. You've probably also experienced happiness of a lesser degree, like when you got extra cash from selling your couch, or finished knitting a sweater, or even after you paid your bills on time.

You work hard to feel good about yourself and make choices you believe are right and good. When you are successful, you feel satisfied, accomplished, proud, joyful, loving, lovable, connected, generous, smart, courageous, and of course, filled with a sense of purpose and meaning.

You knew what would make you feel good, you set out to do it, and it worked. Then that wonderful feeling of happiness arrived. You enjoyed it, savored it, and drank it up.

And then . . . your visit with happiness came to an end.

It's so delightful to go and get what you want (or make sure you do not get what you don't want). But when these pleasurable feelings eventually pass—as everything does—you feel anxious, wondering what you did wrong, or pondering where to find happiness again. Happiness in this form doesn't stay around for long, does it?

But the desire for happiness does stay. So you then try to find something else that will bring it again—a shopping trip, chocolate ice cream, or the excitement of playing the lottery. It doesn't matter that you consciously know the satisfaction won't last. You just want to feel good again—as soon as possible.

Happiness Is a Two-Sided Coin

Desiring happiness can also create another problem—deciding what will make you happy. Sounds like it should be pretty easy, right? Money, love, a good job, vacation, world peace, and health care for all! Unfortunately, the go-get-it path to happiness starts to fall apart when you have two seemingly conflicting desires, such as wanting

- both personal happiness and happiness for all
- both solitude and companionship
- both competition and collaboration

Each option offers something you value that contributes to a more fulfilling life—and happiness. But each desire also requires use of your limited resources: your focus, time, energy, and often money. Turns out, it's not such an easy choice to make.

Take for example your desire for personal happiness. It is natural and built into the human psyche. If you're going after personal happiness, you might get a massage and then work on your art or play in your garden. Your desire for your own private happiness drives your personality (likes and dislikes) and your decisions (choices). There is nothing bad about it or wrong with it.

The desire for universal happiness is also natural and built into the human heart. You might volunteer at a food bank, help a co-worker, or make a donation to your favorite non-profit. It drives your desire to evolve, become a better person, and make the world a more compassionate and loving place—for you and everyone else. There is certainly nothing bad or wrong about that kind of happiness, either.

But there's an inner tension about which one to pursue, and how to make a choice. To end the struggle, people will say one is more important, or more right, than the other. But the desire for universal happiness is not any better or more special than the desire for personal happiness. And personal happiness is not a lesser endeavor than universal happiness. Caring for your own body, mind, heart, and soul *and* caring for others compose the two-sided coin of human happiness.

When you learn how to embrace both kinds of happiness, without valuing one over the other, you discover how they work together to get the results they're each designed to create.

Using Your Personal Resources

Let's move back for a moment to the problem of your resources—and how to use them. You know you don't have an unlimited amount of time, energy, focus, or money, so you have to choose how to best use what you have. How do you decide what's best for you as an individual—and for the collective world at large?

Do you put your focus, time, energy, and money into taking care of yourself and doing what feels good so you can be happy and enjoy your life? Or do you focus on taking care of your responsibilities to others—the kids, the office, your partner, your parents, politics, government, war, poverty, hunger, sex trafficking, oil prices, the economy, the environment, retirement, and on and on—with passion and presence, even if it makes you sick and crazy?

If you don't know how to make this choice, and feel good about it, you can end up feeling dissatisfied, unhappy, insecure, anxious, frustrated, lonely, sad, isolated, and all too often despairing and depressed. Having a happy life is not a simple "go-and-get-it" phenomenon.

So what are you supposed to do? Some folks just flip a coin to decide. But in this book, I'm going to teach you how to consciously make decisions that take into account *both* your desires *and* your responsibilities, so you can begin to experience the happiness you seek.

> Caring for your own body, mind, heart, and soul and caring for others compose the two-sided coin of human happiness.

My Journey toward Happiness

People always ask about my search for happiness—how Ms. Wholesome from middle America came to find this wisdom. It took a while. I explored a lot of options for happiness: numerous handsome and not so handsome boyfriends, exotic lovers, and long-term relationships; a college education; a career in psychology and a specialty in behavioral change; the hope (and constant search) for the security of marriage and a wealthy husband; recognition through public speaking and teaching; service through community organizing; a retreat from altruism into selling encyclopedias and making money in the corporate world. I sang in a church choir, wrote poetry, read books, drew and painted, traveled around the world (nine times), tried out yoga and Pilates, practiced meditation, followed a guru and joined ashram life, studied cooking and baking, had a cat and a dog, and, believe me, there's more!

There was nothing bad in these choices—they made my life richer. But they weren't what I was really looking for.

I was chasing after what I believed was real happiness—joy without sorrow, abundance without scarcity, friends without enemies, acceptance without rejection, trust without doubt, and security without risk—and I was convinced I was right to fight for what I wanted.

I was one motivated girl. I wanted to grab not one, but two handfuls of happiness—just for me—all the time. Still, I didn't want to be obnoxious about it. I was sincere in my efforts and as kind to others as I knew how to be. I worked hard, paid my bills, and supported myself. I just wanted to get married, have a couple of kids, and be happy. But when I didn't get that, I struggled with envy. When others had happiness, I was glad for them—though distressed *I* didn't have it. I kept on trying to grab what I was sure was rightfully mine.

Each activity brought me a taste of happiness. But it never *lasted*. While I experienced amazing aspects of life, I remained mostly unhappy (and very dramatic). I was riddled with the misery of existential angst, stressed, and usually embroiled in some kind of demoralizing emotional turmoil. When the little nasties of hatred, sorrow, criticism, and failure inevitably reared their not-so-pretty heads, I felt crushed, unloved, and unsuccessful.

Eventually, I took the demise of my happiness quite personally. I assumed that my flaws were keeping happiness moving on its merry way—as far away from me as possible. My conclusion: perhaps I didn't deserve to be happy. Sound familiar?

That didn't stop me from still chasing happiness. I saw it as the silver bullet that would eliminate all my problems—forever. The alternative was to feel like a failure or a lost soul—definitely not my goal!

My Silver Bullet—or So I Thought

Around thirty, I decided that psychotherapy and various New Age offerings had failed me. I started combing the spiritual marketplace wanting to devise a clear spiritual practice that would lead me to continual happiness. I was sure I could find it since all spiritual paths seemed to imply that Nirvana, Bliss, Unconditional Love, and Oneness were reachable goals. I just needed the right approach. I tried on different practices like they were clothing, discarding one after the other when nothing really changed inside.

Then . . . I fell in love with the teachings of a guru from India named Osho.

Osho was not only a mystic, but also a philosophy professor. He expounded on Western psychology and the intricacies of the mind in ways I hadn't encountered before. His insights into human psychology left me in awe, and his discourses on emotions were savvy and astute. Sitting in talks he gave to thousands, I swore he aimed his words directly at me and could see into my heart and soul (even though I wasn't sure I had either one).

His physical presence knocked me for a blissful loop, and I was enraptured.

I became a disciple and backpacked my way to Osho's ashram in Pune, India, about a seven-hour train ride from Mumbai. While there, I felt contented and calm. I found relief from my chase after happiness. Osho's presence gave me a mind-boggling taste of "the peace that passes all understanding." I felt alive, full of blissful feelings, and seriously hooked.

Isn't happiness the silver bullet that will eliminate all your problems—forever?

For the first time in my life, I felt whole. Beyond happy, I succumbed to the notion that Osho was the answer to my problems.

Turns out, he was . . . and he wasn't. Osho was the answer because he taught me an important truth about happiness I had missed. And he wasn't because I still had to take what I learned and make it my personal experience, which wasn't always wrapped in joy.

When I returned to my conventional life in Seattle several months later, it was clear my experiences in India had changed me. I was calmer, less dramatic (by a hair), and more able to tolerate discomfort for longer periods of time (a minute and a half now without complaining). I savored the lingering flavor of that peace for eight more years. But again, it didn't last.

By the time I was forty, not even a drop of tranquility remained. I was gripped by my hatred of discomfort, inconvenience, and unhappiness. My greedy hands reached for whatever brought me the most pleasure—usually sex, potato chips, or chocolate, although not always in that order.

I was swept into refueling my pursuit of happiness. But this time, it was exhausting. Instead of having fleeting moments of happiness, as I'd had before my trip to India, I just found sadness, depression, and lethargy. Desperation became my companion. Now I wanted *three* handfuls of pleasure—not just two!

I began to realize I wasn't really in the driver's seat. My conviction that perpetual happiness was attainable was still very real, and I kept fruitlessly trying to find that place where I would be happy and all my problems would be solved—forever.

Then one day, for no particular reason I can remember, I noticed that almost everyone around me was traveling down the same blind alley I was. We were all confused and gathered at its dead end, commiserating on our bad luck, bad karma, or bad choices, but not knowing anywhere else to go.

I wondered if returning to India would once again get me what I needed. But this time I wanted a spiritual awakening that would stay with me, not one contingent on my guru's presence that faded away with time.

A Huge Little Insight

Several months later, while living in Pune again, I was perched on a stone wall outside the ashram. My stomach was busy digesting an overindulgence of naan, hot and fresh out of the ashram's oven. A glorious montage of red, pink, and mauve bougainvillea surrounded me, gracing the dirt road in front of me. Like most roads in India, it was spotted with noisy children playing and middle-aged men seated outside small tea shops, drinking glasses of chai and gesturing wildly as they discussed God and various ways to heaven. The scent of jasmine mixed with the smell of sun-baked cow paddies and roasted peanuts created a slightly pungent breeze.

The exotic smells, each jockeying for dominance, seemed to highlight the confusion churning in my mind. Despite sitting in India, *the* land of spiritual awakening—with a genuine guru to boot—I felt hurt and a bit betrayed by all the advice I'd received and honestly tried to follow. None of it had really worked, and I had been at it for years. I still wasn't happy, blissful, peaceful, or wise.

My heart pulsed with an excruciating sadness. I still hadn't a clue how to be happy, much less what happiness actually was. My soul was slowly starving as I fed it increasingly larger dollops of bitterness and cynicism each passing day. I wasn't aware that I didn't have the complete story about finding happiness. And since I had failed at making happiness last, I began to question the very notion of being happy.

I was trying to make sense of these profound questions when I noticed a familiar old beggar I'd encountered every day. He was walking toward me and, as always, he hailed me with his bright, toothless smile. Eyes shining, he extended his hands palms upward, making his daily request for rupees. Despite his lack of teeth, tattered clothes, and what I judged as demeaning station, his eyes were sparkling with joy, his smile was open and engaging, and his presence emanated peace and calm. As our eyes met, I realized—large, loud, and in neon letters—that for my beggar friend, happiness was obviously not the absence of unhappiness.

Wow! I suddenly realized I defined happiness as the absence of unhappiness. I had defined love as being without hate, joy without sorrow, and security without risk. I realized my way of defining happiness was at the root of my unhappiness. *This* must be the reason I had failed so miserably to capture happiness and make it my own—permanently!

Happiness, Please—Nothing More

After my epiphany, I spent an hour being ruthlessly honest with myself. I realized that in my chasing after happiness, I was simultaneously fleeing unhappiness at breakneck speed. No matter how silly or stupid it sounds, I realized I had fully expected that I could make all unpleasantness simply stop.

I had been trying to build a life for myself that was without sadness, anxiety, despair, anger, rage, shame, ugliness, embarrassment, fear, or depression. When those things appeared, I thought

I couldn't be happy. And if life didn't give me what I wanted (or felt I deserved), I got angry, sad, and frustrated. And, of course, unhappy.

My beggar friend seemed to be living with both happiness and unhappiness. I wondered, "How is he doing it?" I couldn't imagine my eyes shining with joy in that circumstance. Even now, I lose a button on my blouse, and my self-image dives into the toilet. And if my teeth look the least bit yellow, I'm off to the drugstore for the newest whitening toothpaste.

My beggar had to know something more than I did about being happy, and I wanted to know his secret. I had some ideas how to find it. I thought his perspective might be connected to a particular group of folks who are known for their ability to remain unflappable in the presence of distressing circumstances—mystics. With my background in the workings of the mind, I started researching the psychology of mystics to understand how they did it.

Decoding the Secret of Happiness

Contrary to what many think, mystics give very user-friendly advice on how to decode the secrets of happiness and peace of mind. Their wisdom is a special lens that can help you see things differently, and make out what seemed invisible before.

What sets these folks apart from others? Mystics aren't content to live by a theory that says there is something more. And they aren't necessarily concerned about finding a satisfying conceptual understanding of God or the Whole. Instead, they insist on *personal knowledge* through a direct experience of God, Spirit, or the Divine. And as their name implies, they also experience life as a mystery to be lived—not a dilemma to be resolved.

Mystics place their faith in a profoundly personal and *experiential* encounter with the Infinite. That means they trust the felt experiences of their own body more than the intellectual concepts in their mind. They know the existence of something Larger than Self feels undeniably true when it's rooted in a breath-taking bodily experience that can't be explained away.

You may know it, too. I think everyone has had a few brushes with the Divine. But we often don't recognize them as such, or understand what they're about. Experiencing the Infinite blurs our normal sense of separation and reveals that we are both a part of the Whole—and comprise the Whole itself. It's like the magic of a hologram—that sparkly thing you can find in your wallet on your credit cards or driver's license. If you cut a hologram up into pieces, even the tiniest fragment will still retain the whole image.

These personal meetings with God (however you understand that term) often change behaviors that used to feel unchangeable. Perhaps it's because mystics repeatedly experience these meetings that they have a unique psychology. Let's take a look.

Being Unflappable

Instead of acting carelessly, and being led by intense emotions and strong opinions, a mystic's behavior appears peaceful, calm, and accepting—regardless of the situation. Does this mean mystics don't have opinions, feel emotions, or ever act to change things? That they don't feel anger, irritation, or sadness? No, it doesn't. Mystics still take positions, have emotions, and engage in action. But . . . the action is responsive, not reactive. How does it happen?

The mystics' awareness and wisdom temper their opinions and emotions. The mystic remains present to natural reactions, simply allowing them to arise and then pass away. *This is the critical action that opens the space for a more responsive and wiser behavior to appear.*

Being unflappable doesn't mean emotionally flat-lining, disengaging, or letting life pass you by while contemplating your navel. Being unflappable means not losing your cool. You know how to stay centered while fully participating in life, and how to respond to what comes your way rather than react. You can be unflappable by learning how to simultaneously embrace the emotional roller-coaster ride of being human *and* the reflective calm of being divine.

Is It Really Possible for You?

Mystics are subject to the same inner tensions you are, complete with their own personality, personal history, and cultural bias. Life challenges don't simply disappear into thin air just because you have presence and awareness. The secret for dealing with them rests in the way you perceive the challenges.

I found two powerful differences between mystics and the ordinary person when I developed my study of mystic psychology. These are the differences that make the difference and will give you the same freedom to stay happy, centered, and peaceful no matter what. I'll share them with you in detail in the course of this book.

When I learned how to integrate these differences (also part of this book), I discovered an amazing stash of wisdom in the oddest place—my own discontent with life. I hadn't realized that my skepticism and disappointment in life were actually little pieces of wisdom.

> *Life challenges don't simply disappear into thin air just because you have presence and awareness.*

Discontent viewed from a new perspective is actually another route to happiness—one that doesn't rely on having favorable outside circumstances, or being in a pleasant mood already, or always looking on the bright side no matter what. There is wisdom in your discontent. It will lead you to a peace of mind that's very practical and that delivers on its promise to stay with you no matter where you go, what you do, or how you feel.

This may not make sense yet—it is paradoxical. But after you finish reading this book, it will.

I began to apply this new wisdom to my own life by shifting my psychology to match this mystical way of seeing. With the tools you'll learn in this book, you'll learn how to do this too. And you'll discover how to manage the pivotal roles of your unconscious mind, your biology, your brain, and your discontent. That's what this book is all about: *giving you a practical way to embrace this ancient wisdom and make it your very own.*

What Lies Ahead?

In Part One, I introduce you to the essential ideas for living with paradox—mainly, how it is that a truly happy life embraces both the happiness and unhappiness within it. These ideas are the foundation for the changes you will make. We'll shake up the way you see things, and you'll discover how your innate, insatiable, and at times irritating demand for happiness will actually provide the momentum to spur your journey onward.

We will consult with the mystics along the way, who will provide eight guidelines for your journey. You will confront the basic fact of impermanence, an insight crucial to really being happy. Then we'll explore the puzzling predicament of opposites—including how they create our emotional ups and downs—and what to do about it. Finally, we'll discuss the value of learning to manage paradox. You will learn how the contradictions, ambiguities, and the daily dilemmas of life eat up your energy, time, and self-esteem. And you'll learn how to navigate their presence with a calm savvy and a penetrating clarity.

In Part Two, you'll learn how to integrate and practically use the mystical wisdom you discovered in Part One. Over the years my students helped me hone this mystical wisdom into the elegantly simple and effective Facticity® Six-Step Process, which comprises Part Two. You'll learn how to navigate tough choices and approach the notion of happiness and peace in a whole new way. This process is a precise and proven map designed to meet the sophisticated needs of your modern mind—efficiency, simplicity, and clarity—to produce effective results in your everyday life.

> Three crucial facts are impacting your desire to be happy: impermanence, opposites, and paradox.

I've included the stories of two of my most challenging and inspiring students, Maggie and Max, whom you'll meet in the next few chapters. To help you learn, they'll each work through one of their most difficult dilemmas in Part Two using the Six-Step

Process. And you'll have the opportunity to work through one of your basic dilemmas too.

Bear with me if you feel there's a lot of repetition here, because there is. Chalk it up to the need of your *unconscious mind* to hear and/or see things at least seven times before it deems that information relevant to your well-being. I don't want you to walk away from reading this book with nothing more than a nice concept or two for your time. I want your unconscious mind to get its teeth into something it hadn't realized was significant, and leap into action and use it.

Remember: New ideas can change a philosophy, and practical ideas can change a behavior. But most importantly, these are brain-changing ideas that can transform your life. Let's begin.

PART ONE

SOLVING THE HAPPINESS PUZZLE

To be empty is to be full.
—LAO TZU

For it is in giving that we receive.
—SAINT FRANCIS

Be in the world, but not of it.
—JESUS

1
HAPPINESS FROM A DIFFERENT ANGLE

If you're still looking for happiness, you're not alone. An Internet search for it can get you over 100 million results. A search for "wisdom" will produce about the same. Who would have thought being happy and wise could be so elusive? You'd think by now we'd have absorbed the guidance of the multiple traditions handed down through time—spirituality, psychology, philosophy, shamanism, self-development, and even today's Energy Psychology and New Age.

We haven't absorbed it because a fundamental problem makes this guidance less effective than it could be. It's a core confusion that leads us to take sides instead of cooperating to find new ways to make the wisdom practical and accessible.

The essential problem is not the wisdom offered, but how we understand it. Whatever meaning we take away consciously, the *unconscious* mind consistently interprets the wisdom (regardless of how it's offered) as saying this: the solution to our pain and suffering is to permanently establish the positive and the good by permanently eliminating the negative and the bad. That will bring happiness and joy. *This is the crucial issue: our deep misunderstanding of opposites and how to handle them.*

I see this with most people who come to work with me. They are intensely engaged in removing anything bad or negative, but they feel overwhelmed with all it entails—and the unsatisfactory results. Emily is an excellent example.

Chasing After Happiness Is What We Humans Do

Emily, a thirty-eight-year-old supermom, had a handsome, loving husband, three pre-teen kids, a nice home, a career in the medical field, and a way to give back through volunteer work at the homeless shelter. She was convinced this was as good as it got and should have been the key to her fulfillment and happiness. Yet when she came to see me, her stress level was off the charts and anxiety was her constant companion.

One day, desperate for relief, Emily flew into my office, gripping her cup of jasmine tea so tightly I thought she would break it. She flopped into her usual chair and began to cry. "I try my best, but I just can't keep things under control. I can't keep my husband happy, the kids focused on school, the house clean, and my career on track and stay sane. Tell me what I'm doing wrong. I'm sure I could do it better if I just knew how."

Emily isn't alone. She is one of the thousands of unhappy individuals I've encountered in my work who have had the same complaint: "I can't seem to deal with all the choices I have to make every day and be happy. There has to be a better way, doesn't there? My life is driving me crazy!"

And it's not just that Emily has the stress of being a working mom. Emily wants not only happiness, but also wisdom—a practical way to better manage her responsibilities. She told me she wants to stay calm and make decisions without going in circles, worrying if they're right or wrong—decisions such as whether to

- pick up the kids' clothes or leave them lying around for a day
- cook good organic food for dinner or eat out at a fast-food restaurant

- finish that art project sitting in the garage or put it off for another day to take a seminar for her medical career
- have coffee with her friends or hang out at home by herself

Emily goes in circles because she wants to feel good and pick the right choice to get her there. But she's not aware that all of her decisions, big and small, are deeply influenced by something outside her awareness: her *unconscious* mind's drive to feel good, be happy, and choose what will bring maximum good feelings and pleasure. This seems like it should make her happy, right? The problem is, following your unconscious directive to always choose what feels good doesn't always make you happy in the long run.

When you find yourself struggling with an either/or situation, it's your unconscious mind that makes deciding hard. And you may not realize that you're faced with these kinds of decisions all the time:

- Being alone or being together
- Taking care of you or taking care of others
- Being safe or taking a risk

These dilemmas can leave us paralyzed, corner us into arguments, catch us in power trips, make us controlling, debilitate our health, make us lose courage to stand up for ourselves, exhaust us, turn us into workaholics and codependents, block us from choosing our career path, and hook us into other addictive behaviors.

> *An unconscious drive to feel good influences all your decisions.*

All of this is because we don't know how to navigate the flow between opposites and the tension between them— the things that make up dilemmas.

A Different Brand of Happiness Is Available

I'm glad to report there is another way to find happiness and feel good. It still requires you to choose and make decisions (after all, that's human life), but there's a wise way to do it that frees you to feel good about yourself—no matter how bad you feel. Paradoxical? Yes. Impossible? No.

I'm going to map out for you another route to a different brand of happiness—one that doesn't depend on outside circumstances, or whether your body is feeling pleasant or unpleasant emotions.

> You can still feel good about yourself—no matter how bad you feel.

This is very different from the happiness that comes when you get what you want (and don't get what you don't want), the most ordinary go-get-it brand of happiness. It's also not the same as that more mysterious, esoteric brand of happiness that comes for no reason at all.

The focus of this brand of happiness is creating a sustainable sense of peace and calm *in the presence of your own emotional turmoil*, not in its absence. As a bonus, it offers you a wonderful way to travel between the other two brands of happiness.

I introduced Emily to my Six-Step Process, guiding her through the notions and practices you'll learn in this book. Daily challenges didn't disappear, but she discovered how to handle them without the overwhelming anxiety and stress of trying to eliminate everything she perceived as negative or bad.

After using this process for a few months, Emily came back to see me—with a big smile on her face. She shared, "My life's just more workable now. I never thought I could change like this, but now I see things differently and handle things differently. I'm

> Either/or decisions are hard when you don't know how to navigate the flow between the opposites and the tension between them.

not just happier; I think I'm a whole lot wiser, too. And secretly, I'll tell you I finally feel like a real adult."

Most people just want their dilemmas to go away. They have too much to do and too many decisions to make to take time for happiness. Yet, they can't get away from their deep unconscious desire to feel good—and perhaps more problematic, to not feel bad.

Solving the Happiness Puzzle

Not Feeling Bad Is Happiness, Too

Everyone wants to feel good. But is that the same sensation you get when you avoid feeling bad? Your unconscious mind thinks so. In fact, for your unconscious mind, feeling good is survival. It's following our core biological imperative that goes like this: go toward pleasure (keep the species going) and stay away from pain (don't die).

Whatever you choose to do, this imperative always influences your decisions. It becomes problematic when your unconscious mind also applies this directive to your emotions as well. It then forces you to move *toward* emotional pleasure and *away from* emotional pain (which isn't death, but can sure feel like it). This survival imperative makes you believe that not feeling bad will make you happy. The problem with this belief is that you can't get away from pain—physical or emotional—in human life. So no matter how hard you try, you can't avoid the experience of feeling bad.

Life is as tough as it is gracious. It brings each of us a multitude of disappointments. And each distressing turn of events motivates your unconscious mind to once again get you moving toward that impossible goal of never feeling bad (so you can feel good and survive).

> Your unconscious is following a biological imperative: go toward pleasure (keep the species going) and stay away from pain (don't die).

Disappointments Galore

Rationally, you understand disappointment, discomfort, and unhappiness are a part of the package, but your unconscious mind doesn't. So when pain and suffering enter your life, your unconscious mind has to assume you're doing something wrong, someone else is to blame, or God has it in for you, or you'd be feeling good, wouldn't you?

Emily's unconscious mind might say to her: "You know, you're supposed to be able to handle all of these challenges. You must not be doing it right. You should squash that anxiety fast and be calm or your whole life is going to fall apart . . . and then, it's all over!"

Inner dialogues are often kind of melodramatic, with an aura of life and death. When dialogues continue (and they do), you may start feeling frightened because your unconscious mind thinks that feeling bad *is* dying! Avoid feeling bad at all costs.

Your unconscious mind also makes up lots of rules for how to reach its goal of feeling good: "Just do your to-do lists, have positive thoughts, be a good person, save money, be loving, connect with others, become successful, have faith, and cultivate kindness and compassion. Then unhappiness will leave you alone—and maybe you'll even get enlightened, and feeling bad will be gone for good."

These tactics don't work, because your unconscious mind is blind to a huge truth: *you don't get pleasure without pain, positive without negative, or enlightenment (living a conscious life) without endarkenment (living a life without awareness).*

Some paths say living in the middle is the way out of this predicament. But life is both the middle *and* the extremes that create the middle. When you realize you don't get one without the other, the question becomes how to live *with* opposites and the predicaments they create, and still be happy. This book is all about helping you find the answer to that question.

You Cannot *Not* Want to Be Happy

When I heard the notion that, by design, life consists of both pleasure and pain, I thought it was a pretty stupid idea. Really, aren't love and success the answer to happiness, the ticket to a good life?

At the unconscious level, everyone is engaged in a quest for happiness—just like I mentioned at the beginning of the

The unconscious mind is seeking a permanent state of feeling good.

Solving the Happiness Puzzle

chapter. You cannot not want to be happy. No matter where you search for it—food, alcohol, mochas with whip, relationships, children, community, career, hobbies, religion or spiritual path—happiness (and peace of mind) is always the unspoken promise.

The quest is a great motivator, like the proverbial carrot at the end of the stick. But the happiness that comes from getting what you want (and not getting what you don't want) can't deliver what your unconscious mind is seeking—a permanent state of feeling good. Blithely following this path only leads you into that same blind alley I mentioned in the Introduction.

Whether you're aware of it or not, your unconscious desire for survival—otherwise known as feeling good—is always there, influencing your decisions. It works tirelessly to pull you toward certain choices and away from others. And it's also tiring (unless you know how to manage it). I think that's why the notion of heaven (perpetual pleasure and freedom from worry about making wrong decisions) is so appealing. It sounds like you'll be out of that blind alley and no longer have to make choices and decisions all alone—decisions based solely on your own assessment of what's right and what's wrong, what's good and what's bad. You'd be free from those unpleasant inner tugs-of-war in your body that accompany the process of trying to resolve a dilemma.

Sounds just lovely. But unfortunately, that's not how life works.

Emily, like many of my clients, let her newfound wisdom about opposites guide her in a different direction. Her desire to be happy didn't go away, but her way of going after it did. She stepped away from the painful blind alley with the street sign of Perpetual Pleasure. Instead, she accepted that *both* feeling good *and* feeling bad were always going to be a part of her life. Through that, she experienced a deep relaxation. Then she was able to put her energy into finding that different brand of happiness I've been talking about—the kind where you get to feel good about yourself no matter how bad you feel.

> This is the crucial issue: our deep misunderstanding of opposites and how to handle them.

Taking an Alternate Route

Is that same blind alley Emily and I found also in *your* neighborhood? Most of us keep turning into it, again and again, despite the fact that it always leaves us facing a dreary dead-end. The following chapters detail what this blind alley is, how to develop what you need to recognize it, and my precise map for locating the bridge that leads to that different brand of happiness.

This bridge is your alternate route. Actually, it's right there, now, in front of you. But don't worry if you can't see it yet. The next few chapters are going to stir up a few ideas in your head, and then the bridge will appear right there before your eyes, sort of like—dare I say it—magic.

This stirring begins when you recognize that the fabric of your life is comprised of opposites—like success and failure, trust and doubt, or aloneness and togetherness. Opposites are undeniable and unalterable experiences in your life (what I call "facticities"[1]). Not knowing how to handle the tension between them creates your stress. When you understand opposites and how they work—it's like "open sesame." The wisdom of all the ages can flow into your life, granting you that different brand of happiness and peace of mind.

You may not see these opposites yet, but I'll show you how to verify that they do in fact make up the fundamental fabric of daily living. Why is this a life-changing shift? Instead of fighting them, you suddenly see for yourself that the tension between opposites *is* the flow of life. It's where life presents its amazing performances—including the exquisite miracle of you and your journey.

It sounds so glorious!

But there's a catch to getting there. First, your unconscious mind needs an update (from Happiness 1.0 to Happiness 3.0), and your brain (operating

> You don't get pleasure without pain, positive without negative, or enlightenment (living a conscious life) without endarkenment (living a life without awareness).

system) needs an upgrade to run it. The Six-Step Process accomplishes both tasks.

Your Unconscious Mind Needs an Update

Every day your unconscious mind demonstrates its tenacious commitment to wiping out that tension between opposites. It doesn't recognize that tension contributes to life, much less that its presence is the flow of life itself. Your unconscious mind will drive you to spend long hours, lots of dollars, and often an agonizing amount of effort following any path that promises to eradicate or banish the darker aspects of your life. Why does your unconscious mind do this? The biological imperative once again—so you will feel good (and not bad), and thus survive.

You might be familiar with the ways your unconscious operates. It will badger you to transform or transcend your "shadow self" (all the parts of you that you don't like and might even hate). It keeps repeating the same theme: feel good, not bad, and thus survive.

The flow of life is found in the tension between opposites

If you're unfamiliar with the notion of a shadow self, think of it as a gathering of all these parts: loser, fatty, ugly bitch, manipulator, people pleaser, coward, codependent, critic, know-it-all, judge, jury, and victim. You might have unwanted and disliked parts lined up around the block. Some may be resentful, some terrified, and others eager to become different and better. But the unconscious mind won't accept any of them as they are. Change is required!

Unfulfilled Promises

You can spend massive amounts of energy to change yourself . . . for years and years. That's not bad. It's just human.

I spent many decades trying to erase my shadow self by either transforming it so all the darkness in me shifted into light, or transcending it and leaving it behind. With great gusto and hope, I have

- zapped all my "bad" energy with imagined hues of divine illumination
- peeled darkness out of my energy field and banished it from my body and life
- thrown my shadow self up to the heavens for a modern-day makeover
- loved my self-hatred to death in daily morning meditation
- smothered my negativity and chronic complain-itis with gobs of gratitude

I fell under the illusion (so easy to do) that when you get rid of the parts of yourself that make you feel bad, you'll always feel good. But that's not so. Even when you do feel good, your unconscious mind is strong in its commitment. Without hesitation, it continues its mission and re-creates that familiar desire to rid yourself (permanently) of the next set of things you fear, don't like, or simply find unpleasant about yourself, others, and life in general.

Can you change your unconscious mind so it's not like that? No. But . . . I'm going to show you a way to change how you and your brain relate to it so it doesn't keep guiding you down that blind alley. The Six-Step Process shows you how to achieve this, and how to make your life easier—and happier.

Getting to the Land of Unresolvable Dilemma

In my journey toward happiness, many of the personal and spiritual growth programs I used had good results. All that work was not in vain. But nothing removed my despair each time another negative thought appeared in the privacy of my mind, or when I found myself still feeling envious, jealous, angry, or sad. My unconscious goal was to get rid of these things for good. Thus, that sense of failing time and time again never left my side.

I kept on making life into an either/or predicament—over and over, again and again. This is why I kept going down that blind alley. I didn't yet understand that life is lived with the greatest ease when you perceive it as a both/and adventure—happy *and* sad, high *and* low, separate *and* connected, divine *and* human.

Until your *unconscious* mind truly understands the role of opposites and how they create those tension-filled dilemmas that can't be resolved (only managed), you won't be able to see the bridge leading to what I call the Land of Unresolvable Dilemma. This is where you find the wisdom you seek and that different brand of happiness.

First, you have to shift your thinking and perception—shake up your thoughts—and then let them settle in a new arrangement around the three specific experiences I mentioned in the Introduction:

- impermanence (usually called change)
- opposites (often called duality)
- pradox (typically felt as confusion)

Keep reading the rest of Part One to see how you can accomplish these powerful shifts that changed my life and the lives of thousands of my students and clients.

A Touch of Magic

Reorganizing your old ideas into new configurations makes your alternate route—the invisible bridge—suddenly appear before your eyes—presto and alakazam! When you walk across it, the portals to this amazing Land of Unresolvable Dilemma open up and welcome you in. All you need to acquire is a little bit of magic.

Have you ever seen those sci-fi movies where the bad guys skulk around in invisible ships hidden behind cloaking devices? Astonishingly, science now says invisibility cloaks can be a reality.[2] With that in mind, not being able to see what's in front of your eyes may not be just your imagination.

Or maybe you remember spy movies, or fantasy tales, where secret messages were sent with disappearing ink. Or maybe you made disappearing ink as a kid. Then you heated the paper, rubbed it with lemon juice, held it up to the light, or used a special kind of lens to make the hidden words appear.

Let's look through the special lens I'm going to show you in chapter 2. It has just the magic required to get the show on the road.

2
LONGING FOR MAGIC

Desperate to disappear into her cushions, Maggie scrunched her body against the back of her couch. "Why don't I have this figured out?" she moaned to herself. "I'm in my forties and I still don't have my life to-gether." Maggie reached for a tissue from deep inside the nearly empty Kleenex box, sniffed, and loudly blew her nose. "I should be happy and feeling successful by now." Tears streamed down her cheeks and landed on her comfortable old sweater. With resignation, she watched the salty drops of despair melt into the frayed wool. She gave a deep sigh of de-feat. She was overwhelmed by her inability to control her life and make it what she wanted it to be.

Maggie was one of my most interesting, enjoyable, and unhappy students. A forty-two-year-old with a wild hairstyle and quirky personality, she repeatedly traveled the globe working to eradicate poverty and hunger. Maggie was both professional and highly dra-matic. She juggled multiple pathways to misery, relating her tales of disappointment in both love and career with an engaging flair for comedy and tragedy.

The main theme in Maggie's painful vignettes was always the same: she had no idea how to say no when someone asked for her help. Maggie searched hard for happiness, but her inner world always ended up a private hell.

Though Maggie desperately wanted her life to change, she had convinced herself it was impossible. Maggie loved a good magic show. But when she was asked to believe life has real magic, she found herself resistant. She once said, "There isn't enough magic in the whole universe to make my life different."

Now, whether you're pulling a rabbit out of a hat or happiness out of despair, a little touch of magic is essential. I told Maggie that even if the change she wanted felt inconceivable, she could try suspending her disbelief and calling on magic. It can make the impossible possible.

My Six-Step Process has an element of magic to it. This chapter shows you where the magic comes from, and how to find it for yourself, as it introduces you to your mystic's eye, your mind's eye, and the emerging Marketplace Mystic. You'll discover you have a bit of a magician in you as well.

If what you want feels inconceivable, believe in a little bit of magic. It can make the impossible possible.

Let's look at what happened to another one of my clients who also loved magic, but didn't believe it could happen in real life.

The Skeptical Believer

Lawrence, a lean and lanky forty-five-year-old mechanical engineer, came to me when his wife of twenty years decided to change professions. After being a Waldorf teacher for seventeen years, she decided to go into business for herself as an energy healer. He freaked out!

Lawrence was a practical kind of guy. He loved to know how and why things worked. When he wasn't at the office designing and building platforms for offshore oil rigs, he was in his shop behind the house working on his inventions. If he didn't understand something, he either researched the idea relentlessly, or he deemed it silly, sarcastically dismissing it as unrealistic.

Lawrence's wife's account of energy healing couldn't satisfy his demand for scientifically repeatable proof. She found his cynical commentary depressing and felt he squelched her desire to explore the world of energy. Eventually she issued an ultimatum: either stop the negativity, or divorce could become an option.

Lawrence fell into the jaws of a serious dilemma—should he stick with demanding precise proof, or should he pretend he believes in magic to keep the peace? Lawrence loved his wife, but there wasn't anything positive he could say with his extreme negativity toward "energy healing."

Here were his two options: take care of his wife's need for him to support her new career, or stay true to what he believed and maybe lose his marriage. Neither choice felt very good because he wanted to do both. Hence, he showed up in my office looking for help, which, it turned out, came from science fiction.

Stories of magical and improbable possibilities in alternate universes fascinated Lawrence. He was intrigued by how imagined absurdities later became reality. So I asked him to imagine something he found completely absurd.

When I work with clients and students, I often suggest they use their hands to focus on the stress and emotions happening in the body. I instructed Lawrence to place one hand on his forehead and the other on the back of his neck while he thought about his wife's new career. Suddenly, his whole body began to shake in his chair.

"I'm not doing this consciously. What's going on?" he asked. I explained that when he placed his hands in that position and thought of his stress around the issue, his body released the negative emotions that were keeping him from being able to handle his dilemma. This was a first for him. He couldn't explain what was happening. He also couldn't deny it. Maybe his wife's absurd new career had some reality to it after all.

Lawrence may never be a complete believer in the world of energy. His skepticism won't allow it. But the Six-Step Process gave him a taste of the magic of life beyond his logic. When he learned how to embrace both his feelings about energy work and his feelings about his wife, he discovered he could handle this impossible dilemma.

He learned each set of feelings had both strengths and weaknesses. (You'll learn more about opposites, with their strengths and weaknesses, in Step One of the Six Steps.) This gave Lawrence some room to honor and more easily move back and forth between both his wife's need for support and his need to have his own ideas and feelings. I'm happy to report that by learning this process, he saved his marriage.

Lawrence grinned, shook his head side to side, and joked, "It seems like magic, and feels like it too—but I'm not going to say it is!"

The Magic of Mystic Psychology—More Than Just Awareness and Presence

In creating my model of a mystic mindset, I discovered a radically different set of attitudes and assumptions about how life works, and how our role within it works best. It turns out that these viewpoints are precisely what allow the mystic to sustain his depth of awareness and presence regardless of the situation.

The hypothesis in NLP (Neuro-Linguistic Programming) is that if one member of our species does something with excellence, other people can learn how to do it too—from creativity, to making money, to having a good relationship, to being present and aware. That's the purpose of creating a model or map. Since mystics know how to remain unflappable in the presence of unacceptable situations, the Six-Step Process is your map to the same destination.

There are two specific differences in mystic psychology that make the difference. The first is their way of relating to change.

Embrace Impermanence

Mystics embrace change. They embody a deep acceptance of life's ongoing movement and the uncertainty that movement creates. Without this attitude, the reality of impermanence complicates everything, since you can't really count on anything remaining the same.

On the other hand, to stay sane and functional, you have to assume most things won't change: tomorrow the sun will rise and set; time will pass; the day will remain twenty-four hours long; you will eat, work, relate, and sleep; you will take your familiar route to work; and your box of cereal will be where it always is (hopefully).

Do you ever respond to the flow of continual change as an irritating inconvenience? Does it seem like an annoyance you'd like to take over and stop completely? Mystics see it differently. They approach impermanence as an adviser continually informing their thinking and decision-making in the affairs of everyday life. They know that staying tuned to the unending flow of change is invaluable for a workable, happy, and peaceful life.

When you are able to embrace impermanence instead of trying to control it, you'll feel you've found magic. Suddenly you'll have a wise personal adviser keeping you true to the way life works. Your approach to your problems will take a different turn, and you'll be on the road to that different brand of happiness. (You'll learn more about the magic of impermanence in chapter 8.)

> Embracing impermanence—instead of trying to control it—feels like magic.

Embrace Opposites

The second key in mystic psychology is how mystics relate to opposites (or duality). I bet you didn't even know you were relating to opposites. For most people, it's a completely unconscious activity. Because you have a hard-wired biological edict to move toward pleasure and away from pain, your unconscious mind sees opposites as antagonistic forces, with clear winners and losers. Wealth is pitted against poverty, success against failure, and love against hate. One option is right, and the other is wrong.

However, the mystic's unconscious mind perceives opposites as one unified whole moving in harmony. This harmony is actually in the tension between the opposites (there's more on this in chapter 5). It's hidden from normal view, but you're going to learn how to find it too.

For a mystic, this whole flow is by Divine design. It keeps life fresh, new, and balanced. Beginnings turn into endings—then are astonishingly replaced by renewed beginnings.

Can you shift your own psychology to match these two mystical ways of seeing? Your unconscious mind might resist at first, but it will be happy to absorb these two differences—once it understands they are valuable for your survival. Accomplishing these two things is the focus of this book. The work you need to do is simple but not easy. If you're willing to do it, you can learn to do what the mystics do—manage impermanence by creating a bridge between opposites.

> *In mystic psychology, impermanence acts as an adviser, and opposites are perceived as one unified whole.*

A Bridge between Opposites

Throughout Part One, I'll share several mystical guidelines that show you exactly what you're doing and what to do differently. The first guideline comes from the mystic Osho:

MYSTICAL GUIDELINE #1

Intellect divides opposites and makes walls.

Intelligence penetrates opposites and creates bridges.

Up to now, your *intellect* (beliefs and attitudes formed by your culture, religion, education, family conditioning, and probably your genetics) may have been your only tool to help you make sense of life's challenges. But reading this book and using the Six-Step Process activates another tool—your innate mystical *intelligence*— a broader, more encompassing and felt sense of knowing. That's the touch of magic I'm referring to. And there are scientific studies that reveal your brain is already wired for this kind of perception.[3]

Here's a simple way to understand the difference between these two kinds of brainpower:

Intellect divides. Check out your kitchen silverware drawer. You probably have a tray that divides your forks, spoons, and knives, with one left over for your big spoons and little forks, or whatever you want to put there. The creation of those little walls solves the confusion and frustration from having a jumble of silverware just thrown into one drawer. Sections allow you to more easily distinguish fork from knife and spoon. It's efficient and practical—as is intellect.

Intelligence penetrates. Mystical intelligence can see through those walls. Instead of seeing forks, knives, and spoons, it simply sees silverware—objects all made of the same stuff. The distinctions, so useful to the intellect, move into the background; you just see the contents of the drawer as made of one thing. With opposites, mystical intelligence sees through their differences, recognizing them as one whole, moving in a harmonious rhythm back and forth between each other. It creates a bridge between the two, shifting what looked like antagonism into a creative dynamic dance.

Your Mystic's Eye—Seeing, Plain and Simple

Everyone has an inner mystic who can see life in these new ways. I call this kind of intelligence your "mystic's eye." Gently rouse it from its sleep, and you'll discover how it's different from your intellect, or your "mind's eye."

What you usually see is colored by your thoughts and feelings belonging to your mind's eye, or the world of conceptual reality (your intellect). Your mystic's eye sees things through a lens free of logic and emotion (your innate intelligence).

You can think of the mind (concepts and thoughts) like clouds. Clouds are held in the sky. The mind is also held by something larger—an awareness that allows you to perceive your thoughts and feelings. Just like the sky has no borders or boundaries, this awareness is free of distinguishing features. It just is.

Here's the difference between how your mind's eye and your mystic's eye see things: When your mind's eye looks at the sky, it automatically creates a lot of characteristics through comparison. The sky is blue, not red; open, not closed; unlimited, not confined; everywhere, not somewhere; vast, not small; empty, not full; opaque, not transparent; uniform, not varied. This is the world of conceptual reality—life *described* through the lenses of thoughts and words determined through comparing. (Notice all the opposites.)

On the other hand, your mystic's eye simply sees what's there—not what you *think* about what's there. No language is used to describe it. No opposites or comparisons appear. With the mystic's eye, you directly experience things as they are *before* your mind's eye differentiates them by comparing and contrasting shapes, sizes, sounds, colors, tastes, temperatures, and sensations in the body.

The mystic eye is your door to the world of experiential reality. *It is the crucial shift in perception that can change everything.* Have you ever felt the rush of an overwhelming experience—like swimming in the ocean, the birth of a child, a loving connection with your spouse, or grief from a death—before you had words for it? That's part of the mystical experience.

Your Mind's Eye—The Author of Your Story

How you describe what's happening in your life, moment to moment—good, bad, ugly, gnarly, beautiful, scary, or safe—is determined by your personality and training. This comes from your environment, family, cultural norms, national and personal history, and, of course, religion (or lack of it). You put it all together, tie it up with a theme, and this becomes the basis for your story. This isn't bad or wrong; it's human.

But until you discover your mystic's eye, you will assume your mind's eye is telling you the truth, the whole truth, and nothing but the truth.

Maggie's story was sadness and tragedy. Emily's was struggle and strife. You can't live without a story. It gives a sense of meaning and direction, or points out its absence, and it's intrinsic to the development of your personality. But your story is not the final statement about your life, your purpose, or your identity (who you really are).

Your Physical Eyes

Both your mind's eye and your mystic's eye use your physical eyes. Yet, the ways of perceiving are quite different. Think of having two sets of glasses—one that gives everything a certain color (that's the view of your mind's eye), and one with lenses that let you see things clearly, without any tint or hue (that's the view of your mystic's eye). Each set of lenses changes how things look and how they feel. But having *both* is important to leading a happy and peaceful life.

Your mind's eye takes what's there and colors it in a particular way according to your life story. Your mystic's eye sees through what your mind's eye has created and glimpses the essence of what is there behind it. Suddenly, magically, you can see right through what you thought was completely solid and absolutely, unquestionably real—your story. When you see with your own eyes that there is more to your life than your story, it's not just like magic. It is magic.

Learn to look from both your mind's eye and your mystic's eye for a happy and peaceful life.

When Maggie discovered her mystic's eye and learned how to distinguish it from her mind's eye, she was stunned. Quite sweetly, she shared her amazement. "I feel like Dorothy stepping out of her battered house after the tornado dropped it in the Land of Oz. Before, everything was in black and white. Now everything has shifted into color and I'm in a different world." Maggie didn't exaggerate. The shift is small, and yet so mind-boggling that you're pretty much left in awe.

Maggie went on, "My mind's eye still sees my life as a tragic mess. But my mystic's eye sees right through it and shows me both what I lack and what I have. It seems I can see things just the way they are without a problem. It's weird, but I can actually see my life both ways at the same time." She paused and with smiling eyes and a flip of her hair said, "But what's really magical is how much happier I feel—about my life and about me."

Tips for Rousing Your Mystic's Eye

Are you ready to give your mystic's eye a nudge? Here are eight ways to help you explore these different ways of seeing:

Seeing there is more to your life than your story is not just like magic. It is magic.

• Look at a tree directly. Then shift your vision to the space surrounding the tree, its limbs, and its leaves. You can see the tree as a whole or you can see it emerging from the space around it. It looks different depending on where you focus your attention. Keep switching back and forth between the two views.

• Focus directly on an object nearby—a chair, the fridge, or a doorknob—and notice its details. Look at it head on, and then switch to your peripheral vision. That means stay focused on the object with your physical eyes, but switch your awareness to the periphery of your visual range—expand it. You can still see the object, but your peripheral vision gives more information and a much bigger view. Keep switching back and forth.

• Shift your focus from these words on the page to noticing the white space behind them. Keep switching back and forth.

• Imagine your eyes are camera lenses zooming in and out. You'll change your perception of the object you're viewing— but the object remains the same, no matter how the camera shows it to you. Keep switching back and forth.

• TV has two ways available to watch your favorite show: one is regular cable and the other is HD (high definition). See if you can discern the differences and how they impact your enjoyment.

- Look at an object with your normal eyes. Then look at the same object with a magnifying glass. Notice the differences and keep switching back and forth.

- If you're not very visual, do the same practice with sensations in your body. Feel a sensation in a limited area and then expand your awareness to feel more of the body, like moving from an itch on your hand to an awareness of your whole arm, or focusing your attention on your neck and then on your entire upper torso. Keep switching back and forth.

- If your best sensory channel is auditory, tune in to a specific sound. Then expand your awareness to the sounds around it—or the silence behind it. Keep switching back and forth.

Practice each option by going back and forth between the two ways of seeing described. This repetition will lay down a new neural pathway in your brain, helping your unconscious mind more easily use your mystic's eye.

In your normal life, you continually change the way you see things and feel about things a hundred times in a hundred different ways. You can rouse your mystic's eye that easily—and it's an awakening that can profoundly expand your sense of who you really are.

When you open your mystic's eye, you set the stage for finding that different brand of happiness. It may feel a little strange at first, but remember that you're part of an emerging community that is balancing practical life and spiritual life by learning to embrace and manage paradox. The community is made up of what I call Marketplace Mystics.

Over the past decade, the people drawn to work with me began demonstrating a new characteristic: the voicing of a desire to have a private meeting with the Divine that would impact their everyday life:

> Your mystic's eye sees plain and simple. Your mind's eye writes your story. When they work together, they can give you a happy, peaceful life.

- "I want my daily life to be my spiritual life."

- "I want to know there's more to life, not just believe there is."
- "I want to experience the peace that passes all understanding"
- "I want to find God in my body."

Having a personal relationship with the Divine—that bigger force—is a key for mystics, and it's a very individual experience.

If you're pulled to this book, there's a good chance you may also be an emerging Marketplace Mystic. If so, the question is, Are you aware of it?

Following are some ways you can determine whether or not you belong to this community.

The Emerging Marketplace Mystic

Marketplace Mystics don't live in a monastery or an ashram, and don't usually have time to practice sitting in meditation four to six hours a day. Instead, they (and you) live and participate in the global marketplace. If you're like these Marketplace Mystics, you work, raise your family, have hobbies, go grocery shopping, watch TV and DVDs, cook, save money for retirement, try to be a good person, aim to meditate at least five to ten minutes a day, and have a growing appreciation of life as a mystery. You feel a pull to more fully embody your spiritual values in daily life, and do your part, however small, to make the world a better place.

Here are some additional characteristics. You certainly don't need all of them. Try them on for size to see if they fit you:

- You rejected, or lost connection with, your childhood religious or spiritual upbringing.

- You remain frustrated by your desire to find God or Spirit through the mind or intellect.

- You think you may have a penchant for something like mystical thinking but want to continue enjoying the comfort and convenience of marketplace living.

- You have a strong sense of dedication to making our world a more humane place to live.

- Monastic living or surrender to a guru-driven lifestyle isn't of interest to you.
- You desire to bring a spiritual understanding into your daily life through conscious living and understanding from the heart.
- You hold the external world and its challenges as equally important to the internal world and its challenges.
- You envision bringing social, political, and spiritual potential into a seamless and creative partnership.
- You want to live more consciously with awareness of each moment's mystery, understanding and accepting your role within it.
- You desire to open your heart, expanding your capacity for compassion.
- You want to know how to behave as both a human being and a divine being simultaneously—at the office, at home, and in the privacy of your mind.
- You want to know what this thing we call the Divine actually is but are frustrated by lack of words and/or experience.

If any one of these traits describes you, you are likely a Marketplace Mystic and *Unflappable* can help you further integrate your spiritual values into the everyday world, bringing greater balance and peace of mind.

What Is the Divine, Anyway?

The question, What is the divine? can't be answered by anyone but you. Everyone's relationship to the Whole is the same—and yet uniquely different. The Divine, however you describe it—Mystery, God, Source, Presence, Spirit, Love, Light, Christ Consciousness, Awareness, Suchness, the Universe, the Infinite, and many more— is always hiding out in your daily life.

When you step aside from your mind's eye (your story about what's happening) and use your mystic's eye alone, you can find it—paradoxically—hiding openly in secret places like:

- the sound of a dog's bark in the still, early hours of the morning
- the feel of heat on your fingers from a steaming cup of coffee or tea
- the sight of a leaf gracefully falling from its branch to a new home on the ground
- the fragrance of freshly cut grass permeating the heat of summer days
- a glimpse of your beloved's sweet innocence as he sleeps
- daybreak spreading itself across the morning sky

Perceiving the mysteriousness of such simple events makes the magic of life evident. The mind becomes boggled into silence, and the "peace that passes all understanding" gently rises.

Have you had this experience? Do you want it again? More often? Or does it simply sound beyond your reach? It's not. It is yours to enjoy as often as you wish. You just need that little bit of magic. And now you know where to find it—your mystic's eye— the second most important thing to take away from this book. The first is coming right up in the next chapter.

Using your mystic's eye will slow down your chase after happiness, and you'll notice something has also been chasing after you. Wonder what it is? Read on.

3

THE WISDOM OF YOUR DISCONTENT

Max rushed into the sunroom, his Armani suit jacket flapping, snatched his designer briefcase from the table, and began searching for his keys. Suddenly he stopped. His eye caught the brightly colored curtains blowing through the open window, fluttering like the beating of his heart. Max trembled. Successful, yet unhappy and scared, he slumped his shoulders as his customary self-confidence deflated. In that private moment, Max knew he was a failure.

"Stop it!" he shouted aloud. "Failure can't be an option." The sound of his voice snapped his shoulders back into place. He grabbed his keys off the table and flew out the door. Climbing into his silver Lexus, he let the soft, gray leather welcome his body. He took two deep, purposeful, breaths, pushed the whole problem aside, and switched his focus to where he felt safe and secure—work. He flipped on the radio and let the genius of Mozart surround him. As he started rehearsing his upcoming talk, the quandary of whether he was a success or a failure quietly drifted away.

Working with Max was delightful. His self-deprecating humor let me glimpse his well-hidden vulnerability and fear of failure, and his big heart wouldn't stay concealed behind his professional façade—or his six-foot frame.

At thirty-five, Max was a well-established inspirational speaker. His specialty was The Keys to Happiness—at Work and at Home. But off stage, happiness wasn't his companion. He was too busy nailing down success—serious business for Max. Despite his established reputation, just thinking of failure shriveled his confidence and self-esteem.

Max inspired others to seek happiness by staking their claim on his idea of success: a snazzy car, designer clothes, access to private jets, a country club membership, travel to exotic places, gourmet foods, a haircut every two weeks, an attractive spouse, kids in private school, a boat, and a showplace house with a garden. What more could you ask for?

His strategy for success was simple: avoid failure and you'll succeed. However, Max's outer success didn't quell the sense of failure reverberating through his inner world. His keen focus on avoiding failure didn't make him feel very accomplished, or happy, although it seemed a viable route to success. By all counts, he had two of the possessions we all desire most—health and wealth. Wisdom and happiness were still up for grabs.

He was not aware of the unalterable and undeniable nature of opposites: they travel together and are inseparable. Where one goes, the other follows. This means Max's success would inevitably be followed by failure, or feelings of failure, somewhere in his life. He sensed this, and it frightened him.

> The nature of opposites can't be changed. Where one goes, the other must follow.

Embarrassment and shame about failing, including making the simplest of mistakes, forced him to try to cover it up or deny it. As a result, he started feeling like failure was actually chasing after him! He just wanted to be happy; instead he felt unhappy and scared—and deeply puzzled.

The Happiness Puzzle

Have you ever scattered all the pieces of a jigsaw puzzle on a table so you could put them together more easily? While you may prefer to start with a certain kind of piece over another, it wouldn't make sense to throw away the puzzle pieces that didn't appeal to you at first. Say the puzzle was a photo of an amusement park, and you didn't like the part where a guy is guzzling beer, or the roller-coaster piece that reminds you how sick you got last time you rode one. That may be so, but without those pieces on the table, you'd never see the whole picture. There would always be holes where those pieces fit in.

In real life, it's the same. You throw away the pieces that don't appeal to you to avoid what you don't want. You can't see the whole puzzle picture of happiness without all the pieces of the puzzle. Yet, none of us wants to bring those pieces back. The ones we throw away relate to our discontent with life.

For most of us, this is not a happy realization. All the same, let's assume you find the courage and willingness to bring these undesirable pieces back anyway and put them in their proper places. You then discover there's still one piece missing—unraveling the baffling nature of paradox. (The next chapter is all about that). But first there's a catch to finding this missing piece. You have to deal with your discontent, because that's where this last puzzle piece is hidden.

Discontent comes in all shapes, sizes, and colors. For Max, it was failure. For Maggie, it was tragedy. For Emily, it was despair. Is your discontent your creation? Or could it be by design and with some purpose?

Rain, Rain, Go Away—Please Don't Come Another Day

Shortly after Max came to see me, I introduced him to a simple yet profound piece of mystical guidance from Sengsten (or Sosan Zenji), the Third Zen Patriarch of the Zen Buddhist tradition. This is the number one piece of guidance I want you to remember from reading this book. Sengsten offers a very practical observation as seen through his mystic's eye.

MYSTICAL GUIDELINE #2

To set up what you like against what you dislike
is the dis-ease of the mind.

This is what Max and Maggie have been doing! When you follow a strategy for happiness (or success) that doesn't work, you generate stress and frustration (dis-ease) in your mind and body. Sengsten went on to say,

> *When the deep meaning of things is not understood,*
> *the mind's essential peace is disturbed to no avail.*

When I told Max this, he said, "I never thought about why I want success. But now that I think about it, I guess it's because I do want some peace of mind—you know, that someday I'll have enough money and security to take time to just rest, give up worrying, and enjoy life and my family."

Everyone wants a sense of ease with life—a way to make the daily grind less frustrating and less stressful for your mind, heart, and soul. But setting up what you like against what you dislike only creates dis-ease.

Max hungered for success and freaked out at failure. He clung to one and avoided the other—and was continually anxious. We all do this, and, truth be told, it simply doesn't work in the long run. Do you focus on success, or one of a hundred other desires? Here are a few of the most common ones:

- Love
- Connection
- Recognition
- Wealth
- Freedom
- Closeness
- Companionship
- Self-expression

- Knowledge
- Security

Check It Out for Yourself

Take a few minutes and write down something you want. It could be money, or a relationship, or a new couch. Remember, your unconscious mind filters everything down until it gets to a set of opposites at the bottom. (It has to decide whether it will bring pleasure or pain.) So if you wrote down *money*, ask yourself what you'll have when you get it. Maybe you're really after things like wealth, security, or freedom. These all have obvious opposites. Money doesn't.

With a relationship, ask what you get when you have one—things like connection, togetherness, or companionship. Again, these all have obvious counterparts. A relationship doesn't. The same goes for that new couch. Ask what it will bring to your life—things like beauty, comfort, pleasure.

Now write down the opposite of each thing you want. When Max did this exercise, he said he wanted success, winning, and courage. For the opposites, he wrote failure, losing, and cowardice. I asked him what he felt in his body when he looked at each polar pair. Did he feel a pull toward one? A push away from the other? Or nothing at all?

Surprised, Max said, "I don't feel any pull toward the positive things I'm after. But I do feel a strong aversion—almost repulsion—away from the negative things. Does that mean my unconscious mind is really doing what you're talking about, focusing completely on avoiding the negative?" Max couldn't quite believe his own body—but bodies don't lie.

Check how you feel in your body. You may indeed feel pulled toward the thing you want, or repulsed by what you don't. If you feel balanced, there's no problem for you with this particular polar pair. But if you're pulled toward the positive, or away from the negative, so far that your body practically falls over, there's an aversion to the opposite hiding somewhere in your unawareness.

Please don't judge what you find one way or the other. This is just an exploration, a way to learn what your unconscious mind is doing with the polar pairs it encounters every day. And even though we can't change your unconscious mind's process, the mystics have a little paradoxical trick that magically alters what can't be changed. Hang in there. It's a secret strategy—and that's what the Six-Step Process is going to teach you how to do.

Whatever it is you're after, remember the promised ROI (return on investment) is always your happiness—and now you can include something your unconscious mind also wants—to peacefully engage in problem solving.

Your Mind Wants Peace, Too

Your mind has the capacity to peacefully and easily do its job—finding problems and solving them. Your mind works a lot like your stomach, which can do its job—digest your food—peacefully and easily (and more effectively) if you eat the foods that are best for your system. For the mind, setting up what you like against what you dislike is like feeding your stomach a steady diet of deep-fried food. It gets upset and can make you nauseous.

Shake up these ideas: impermanence (usually called change), opposites (often called duality), and paradox (typically felt as confusion).

You can't find happiness and peace of mind by trying to create a life *without* unhappiness—or by *only* feeling good and *not* feeling bad. You need a strategy that works for you and for your mind.

First, understand your unconscious mind is creating the difficulty because it has defined happiness as the absence of unhappiness. Second, develop the knack for that different and life-changing brand of happiness that can stay with you no matter where you are, what you're doing, or how you're feeling.

The key is learning how to embrace opposites rather than setting them up one against the other. The Six-Step Process will teach you precisely how to do that. But first you have to shake up those ideas we talked about in the introduction.

The Route to a Different Brand of Happiness

We can begin shaking up these ideas by checking out Sengsten's guidance. In everyday language, Sengsten is telling us that reaching for the good stuff and avoiding the bad stuff is not a workable plan. You can see how we all do this if you look at current self-help advice. The majority of it sets up what you want against what you don't want.

For instance, it tells you to bring your shadow self out into the light, encircle it, and heal it using tools like positive thoughts, imagining goodness infusing your every move, etc. Manifestation gurus say you'll get jobs, money, relationships, and success if you are positive, imagine what you want already having happened, feel it as if it's already here, and avoid being negative at all costs.

The unspoken promise is you'll permanently get rid of "the dark"; it will stop chasing after you, and you'll find peace, joy, happiness, and love—always.

Your *unconscious* mind creates a Disney-like movie: birds will sing, hearts will explode, the sun will shine *every day*, and bank accounts will overflow. All ignorance and darkness will be *banished*. Poverty disappears. Holes fill up with love and light, and you live "happily ever after."

Grasping for the good stuff and avoiding the bad stuff isn't a workable strategy.

If only it were true.

Most self-help offerings fail to deliver these Disney-like promises. That's not because personal-growth processes are wrong; they're just misleading. They don't tell you the rest of the story about how to be happy and peaceful. (However, you can still help manifest what you want. It's actually part of your job. I'll clarify this seeming contradiction in chapter 8.)

We're all trying to solve the brainteaser of the happiness puzzle, whether we're aware of it or not. Let's take a look at the discontent we're trying to banish. Remember, it holds the missing piece of the happiness puzzle—paradox.

Your Wisdom Is Chasing After You

For me, realizing life consists of both pleasure and pain, *by design,* and it is possible to have happiness despite this, was a revelation. As I put the pieces together, I realized my nagging feelings of dissatisfaction, that little dissenting voice that made me feel like I wasn't in the right place at the right time, or doing the right thing, was all a set of instructions for how to find inner peace in the *presence* of my emotional turmoil. All this time, I'd been chasing happiness—and my discontent had been chasing me. This race had gone on for years, and I'd had no idea.

Instead of living life to banish negativity, turn around and look at what's chasing after *you.* Whether your negativity, dark side, shadow self, or discontent arrives as irritation, anxiety, negativity, fear, dissatisfaction, disillusionment, disappointment, disconnection, or despair—or more intensely as anger, rage, blaming, aggression, and hatred—it carries a profound wisdom: the wisdom of your discontent.

What's chasing you is the wisdom of your own discontent.

However it appears, or whatever you name it, embracing your discontent is a direct route to a relaxing and clarifying piece of life's wisdom. It's been chasing after you since you first said, "Life isn't fair!" Perhaps the polite thing to do is invite it for a cup of tea and listen up.

Your Wisdom

Let's back up for a moment. What is wisdom? Even with all your faults, problems, and mistakes—like spending $150 for lunch, frittering away hours on Facebook, or telling your boss, to his face, that he's a jerk—you have wisdom. Do you freak at the notion *you* have wisdom? Don't. Everyone has it.

Simply defined, wisdom is a smart way to use what you know *in a practical fashion.* When it's pouring rain, you reach for your raincoat and/or umbrella before you go outside. You use what you know (rain is wet and will soak you to the bone) in a practical way (you should cover up). When you see your car's gas gauge hover over E, you use what you know (your car is going to stall soon) in a practical manner (you pull into the gas station and fill up).

Wisdom is your natural ability.

> *Wisdom is a smart way to use what you know in a practical fashion.*

The Wisdom of Your Discontent

You may expect to get wiser as you grow older. But wisdom doesn't come just in expected ways. Your discontent has some to give you, too. Your discontent isn't chasing you because it wants to punish you or teach you a lesson. You haven't failed at life, and you're not a bad person, or unworthy, or intrinsically defective. Discontent is just life's most direct way to get your attention.

You may not have noticed the wisdom in your discontent yet—maybe you haven't even been present enough to see, hear, or feel it calling your name. But discontent is a messenger, and it says, "Embrace me—not for the purpose of transcending, transforming, or banishing me from your life, but to receive my wisdom. A roadmap is tucked inside me, and it will lead you to life's gift of inner peace."

Let's see how one of my clients embraced the wisdom of her discontent—and how it helped her reach her seemingly outrageous goal of "the peace that passes all understanding."

The Tough, Ball-Busting Lady Vice President

At forty, Josey found herself a very successful VP at one of the largest banks in the industry. Her stardom within the company rested on her ability to accomplish things in a no-nonsense manner. She managed tasks and relationships efficiently and effectively. The problem wasn't Josey's reputation on the outside; it was her inner struggle creating stress and unhappiness.

When she came to see me, she said, "I want relief. I need some of that 'peace that passes all understanding.'" When I heard this, I laughed and commented, "That's quite an order." She chuckled too, although Josey was very serious. She deeply disliked her work persona, even though it brought her success, a good living, and a sense of accomplishment. She wanted to change, but she didn't know how.

As a youth, Josey was a staunch political activist and lived out her convictions with courage. She grew up in Canada, and when she moved to the United States, she couldn't find the same hotbed of political activism that brought her alive and instilled meaning and purpose. She focused on daily life instead and started working as a bank teller. She flew up the corporate ladder and earned a reputation for being a tough, ball-busting boss. This had brought her success, but now she was paying the price: she was exhausted, distressed, and anxious.

Josey longed for a reprieve, but she couldn't let go of being tough—even though she hated it. Being sweet and soft meant giving up her toughness and strength—and her political views and activism. She'd tucked away the soft side of her personality long ago in order to wage war on the side of what's "right"—and to survive.

Now her discontent (anxiety, stress, and fear) was signaling her to pay attention. Listening to it made her realize she wanted to follow the sweet softness of her heart—as long as she could somehow remain tough and strong and keep her job.

I taught Josey how to use the Six-Step Process to explore the opposite of the tough persona she clung to. Through her mystic's eye, she perceived softness in a new light, and its value and strengths were revealed. She could see that tough and soft were not at odds with each other; they could coexist peacefully and harmoniously. It was a contradiction Josey was glad to embrace, and it led her to a more workable life and that different brand of happiness.

As Josey integrated softness into her work persona—and the rest of her life, too—she shared the following: "Having my heart open in this new way makes each day more worthwhile and meaningful—and, fun! And I love having so much more peace of mind!'

The Wisdom of Your Discontent and Opposites

The wisdom of your discontent shows you precisely how and why life flows between opposites. It gives you a fresh perspective on how life uses opposites to create balance. And it guides you to living a life with joy, love, and happiness.

Understanding the purpose of your discontent means you can stop running, seize your courage, turn around, and face your unhappiness head on. Not to transcend or transform your discontent, but rather to embrace it, relax into it, and allow its wisdom to infuse your life.

Why would you want to face and embrace what every fiber of your body wants to run away from? It might sound like the last thing you'd want to do—until you find the same relaxation Josey found. And that comes with finding that final missing puzzle piece called paradox.

Paradox: The Last Piece of the Happiness Puzzle

You've seen most of the big picture now. You've learned that:

- Happiness is not the absence of unhappiness.
- Setting up what you like against what you dislike creates dis-ease in your mind.
- You have a mind's eye and a mystic's eye.
- Your discontent is a messenger and has wisdom for you to gather and use.

- The wisdom of your discontent can lead you to a different brand of happiness.
- You have to shake up your existing ideas around opposites, impermanence, and paradox in order to see the wisdom in your discontent.

We'll get to the details of opposites and impermanence in chapters 5 and 8. But the last puzzle piece putting it all in place is paradox. You'll recognize it because it has a picture of an infinity loop, the universal symbol for what is never ending—in this case, life flowing between opposites: from here to there, from this to that, and back again.

Embrace your discontent and receive its wisdom.

The wisdom of your discontent can guide you to that different brand of happiness by showing you how to manage paradox, rather than trying to get rid of it.

The next chapter shines some light on what paradox is, how it's affecting your life, and what to do with it.

4

THE BEWILDERING NATURE OF PARADOX

Maggie chomped down hard on her fingernail and chewed away. She watched the rain glide down the windowpane, the drops like tiny mirrors reflecting her tears. Hoping some secret guidance would shimmer forth, she muttered about the messy situations waiting for resolution. "I have to figure things out—make decisions. My life is crumbling, and I don't know how to stop it!" She reached for her shawl and wrapped it around her long legs as she slung them over the back of her couch. "My career, my finances, my friendship with Eleanor, my relationship . . . Oh my God, nothing will work out." She had no clue how to make the decisions she had to make. Feeling trapped and stupid, Maggie sighed, pushed them all out of her mind, and made one decision that was easy: a cup of that new herbal tea—and perhaps just a few potato chips. Maybe that would help.

Maggie frequently arrived at our meetings feeling overwhelmed and depressed. She didn't know she was caught in the grips of a common paradox we've all encountered—wanting to please your friends and family *and* yourself *at the same time.*

When two opposite desires simultaneously arise, they each generate opposing actions (such as having lunch with your friend, or staying home alone and doing your own thing). You can't fulfill both at the same time. Efforts to balance them by doing one and then the other don't relieve the anxiety of the situation or lower your stress level. Why? The situation keeps returning, and you have to re-decide again.

This chapter introduces you to your familiar but unnamed experience of paradox. We'll explore a core paradox—human versus divine—its conflicting guidelines, and how the Six-Step Process harnesses the power of your biology to balance the two. First, let's get clear on what paradox actually is.

What Is Paradox?

You face paradox any time you're confronted with two opposite desires existing at the same time that don't *logically* go together. Things like hating someone you love, slowing down in order to hurry up, doubting someone you trust, and feeling sad when you're happy, or lonely when you're with friends.

You feel conflicting desires in your body as an inner tug-of-war. This is paradox in action.

Logically, you can only feel or do either one or the other. You can't do or feel both at the same time. Yet, you do experience conflicting desires and emotions in your body all the time. And just like Maggie, you feel them as that inner tug-of-war. This is paradox in action, whether you're aware of it or not.

The Missing Piece to the Happiness Puzzle

Most of us aren't able to solve the whole happiness puzzle because we're busy fixing the one puzzle piece we believe is causing the problem. In fact, we may not even remember there is a whole picture until we get fed up with failing to fix our lives.

Paradox is the puzzle piece you don't even know is AWOL. Paradox isn't something you can solve and get rid of for good; it is a basic human predicament to *manage*, not fix. And it is perplexing, because you oftentimes won't even know when you're struggling with paradox, much less know to discuss it or explore it.

Paradox permeates our daily life problems. It appears when we're faced with the dilemma of two simultaneously arising desires. A dilemma limits you to only two choices. You're faced with choosing either one desire or the opposite desire because logically, you can't do both. That never feels good. Choosing one and not the other makes you feel you've lost something you wanted—just like Maggie did.

> Paradox permeates our daily life problems.

Common Dilemmas

Have you ever felt any of these common dilemmas?

- Should you go out and have a good time with your friends? Or should you stay home and repair the fence that needs mending? You feel the desire to both work and play. How do you choose?

- Should you put that bonus check into your savings account so you reach your monthly savings goal? Or should you spend it on the new iPhone that would make your life easier? You feel the desire to both save and spend. How do you choose?

- Should you spend the evening with your partner as he or she asked? Or should you follow your own desire for being alone? You feel the desire to fill both your partner's need to be together and your own need to be alone. How do you choose?

There are hundreds of common daily dilemmas that we struggle to resolve permanently every day (chapter 6 helps you identify these dilemmas). You want both options, but you *have* to choose one—hopefully without feeling

- guilty
- you've missed something
- you've done something wrong
- you've hurt someone you love
- you're a bad person

There's one particular dilemma that underlies most of our struggles. It's the most difficult human pickle there is—being *both* human *and* divine.

The Predicament of Being Both Human and Divine

On the one hand, we are born, play, work, love, grieve, and exist in a human body with frailties and irritations, sensations and passion. On the other hand, we have questions about what happens before birth and after death. Are we more than our human existence? What happens when we step back from daily struggles to experience a bigger picture?

Because life is bigger than our ability to grasp it, try as we might, we often rely on beliefs to soothe these difficult existential questions. Still, the mystery of it all—and the question of our place in it—never really goes away.

The problem starts when we see being human as flawed, and being divine as perfect. Then we don't know how to live with, let alone relish, being alive on this earth. We race to experience the spiritual—*Ahhhhhh!*—then crash into the irritation of being human—*Aarrgh!*

Happiness in Two Dimensions

To understand the irritations of being human, you need to realize that there is one basic unfulfilled desire at the heart of human discontent: the desire to have life be the way you want it to be.

> Discontent rests in wanting things to be what they're not.

Yet . . . wanting things to be what they're not motivates our dreams. This desire marks us as human, so how can this be a problem?

If you don't put your energies into making your dreams come true, you feel unfulfilled and dissatisfied—whether those dreams are baking a tasty cake, throwing a party for your partner, writing a new song, making the world go green, or inventing the next technological leap.

Humanness

At the human level, discontent drives our dreams. Picture yourself as a dream machine designed by Divine Decree to dream. In fact, you cannot not dream. Happiness for the human dimension is actualizing your dreams, bringing what isn't yet real into reality.

Spiritualness

From the spiritual perspective, you're a child of God, perfect as you are, and resting in Buddha Nature, Christ Consciousness, or Love and Oneness. In effect, the essence of you is ultimately divine and perfect as is. No change needed, and no dreams desired.

Happiness for the divine dimension is enjoying the present, "being here now," and going with the flow.

How can you be here now *and* run after your dreams? The answer is learning how to manage paradox. Then you'll stop trying to get rid of that unpleasant inner tug-of-war by chasing the dimension that's right (usually divine) and avoiding the dimension that's wrong (usually human). You discover your inner tug-of-war has a vital role to play; then you're free to be present to the moment while you're also pursuing your dreams.

Discontent rests in wanting things to be what they're not.

Bewildering Advice

Being both human and divine generates some confusing and paradoxical guidelines. You've heard them all but may not realize how they influence the way you live, make decisions, and try to resolve your dilemmas.

| Human Self | Keep moving and go after what you want |
| Divine Self | Stay still and be grateful for what is. |

| Human Self | Focus on the future and expect to get what you want. |
| Divine Self | Focus on the present and let things be as they are. |

| Human Self | Heal your wounds from the past. |
| Divine Self | You are perfect as you are. |

Without the wisdom of your discontent to manage these paradoxical directions, *your* unconscious mind has to decide which guideline is the right one to follow—since you logically can't do two contradictory actions at the same time. It will move you toward the one it thinks is right and away from the one it thinks is wrong. Here it is again! Setting up what you like against what you dislike.

Check It Out for Yourself

Take a minute right now and ask yourself which of the above guidelines your unconscious mind is trying to follow. How will you know? Simply check out what you think and feel. Do you believe one is right and the other wrong? Does one dimension seem irrelevant to your happiness? Do you find yourself desperately trying to move back and forth between the two without any reliable way to decide which to choose? Do you find yourself second-guessing your decisions time and again? Remember, don't judge. This is just an investigation. Be lovingly ruthless. No one else needs to know what you find. It's just between you and the lamp post.

> *Tension and distress are a natural part of the human experience.*

The Happy News

Now here's the happy news. Whatever you find, you can relax. Your system is operating as it was designed, automatically responding to life's dilemmas by deciding which option will bring pleasure and which option pain.[4]

But shoot—you're still not happy.

However, you can be happy when you add paradox—the missing puzzle piece. You can make sense of your suffering, reduce it, and create a workable life. How? You realize that your experience is right on:

You are *both* human *and* divine simultaneously. That's the paradoxical nature of your predicament. You are both at once, living a life of tense relaxation and stressful peace—or perhaps more appealing, a life of relaxed tension and peaceful stress.

Wait a minute! Did that just feel like a jolt to your brain? What the heck does that mean?

Happiness and inner peace come by experiencing them both—without making one better or worse than the other. What makes this difficult to reach is actually your biology, which is the source of much of your emotional struggle.

> Relaxation and peace are a natural part of the divine experience.

The Wisdom of Biology and the Wisdom of Your Discontent

The wisdom of your biology (to make sure you survive) can incorporate the wisdom of your discontent (to make sure you are happy, peaceful, and living a workable life). Dr. Bruce Lipton, creator of *The Biology of Perception* video, sets the stage.

In his YouTube videos, he explains that genes in all of your cells are programmed to do two things: either grow or protect. The cell can either be in growth mode (moving toward positive signals or nutrients) or in protection mode (moving away from negative signals or toxins). Yes, that's right. The whole physical system is set up on an either/or basis, like an on/off switch, not a dimmer mechanism that flows between on and off. The more protection the cell determines it needs, the less growth it can make. No matter what, it's all about survival. Sound familiar?

Your unconscious mind is simply following the patterning of your physical cells. However, this doesn't work so well for emotional and psychological survival: only being able to move toward the positive and away from the negative isn't a successful strategy for happiness, peace of mind, and a healthy sense of who you really are. This makes your poor old unconscious mind quite confused.

Paradox helps you make sense of your suffering, reduce it, and create a workable life.

Your unconscious mind needs a better way, which is what this book provides.

Although your cells may not be designed to both grow and protect simultaneously, you are. This is the magic of human consciousness.[5] And the essence of mystic psychology.

That Little Bit of Magic

Dr. Lipton also says that "perception rewrites genes"; that means how you perceive things can affect change in your biology, brain, and behavior. The way your mystic's eye perceives gives your unconscious mind an alternate way to determine what's good and what's bad—and thus what's best for survival. It provides a new option or strategy for finding that different brand of happiness.

The Six-Step Process installs this new option in your neurophysiology.[6] It guides your unconscious mind to move you toward embracing the paradox of both feeling good and feeling bad as the best strategy for emotional and psychological survival.

This means it will also begin to move you away from setting up what you like against what you dislike. (If you have objections to this idea, I promise they'll be addressed a little later on.) This is what the Six-Step Process accomplishes. You're still moving toward and away, in line with your biology's prime directive—survival. But now you're free to live life as a both/and adventure rather than an either/or predicament.

Harnessing Biology's Prime Directive

You can't change this prime directive for survival (moving toward and away). Remember, it's hard-wired in your brain. But the Six-Step Process skillfully uses the power of this biological drive for survival to send your unconscious mind in a new direction.

Instead of pushing you toward pleasure and away from pain, your unconscious mind gains the additional option of embracing both.

The current choice is either move away from pain or toward pleasure.

The new choice is

- either move away from *setting up what you like against what you dislike* because it creates dis-ease—and that is threatening to your survival,

- or move toward *embracing both what you like and dislike* because it is the optimal way to feel good—and survive.

With this new option in place, Maggie began to understand paradox, how it permeated her daily life—and how to manage it. Her long-lost hope for a better life came back for a visit. And she stopped blaming herself when she realized her biology was the deeper issue. Let's look at how embracing paradox helped another of my clients shift his view of the world.

The Spiritual Teacher Who Hated Being Human

Joachim was a very round, jolly, and intense fifty-three-year-old spiritual teacher. He came to see me because he felt stalked by confusion and anger. Being a spiritual teacher, he didn't feel comfortable talking about his problems with family, friends, or parishioners. But it was clear to me that his unconscious mind's drive for survival was influencing his understanding of his spiritual path.

Joachim taught the Kabbalah, a Jewish mystical path intended to explain the relationship between the infinite (God) and the finite (you and me). He had heard the fundamental teaching as "human emotions are bad, and Spirit's wisdom is good."

"I can't seem to get people to ignore their emotions. Emotions keep us from God and create pain and suffering. They're the devil in disguise. Listening to Spirit brings happiness and joy, without suffering. I feel like I'm failing everyone because they're not further along in their spiritual development. I must be doing something wrong. Sometimes I think I should give up teaching altogether."

To make sure he survived, Joachim's unconscious was setting up what he liked (Spirit's wisdom) against what he disliked (human emotions) and then clinging to what was pleasant and escaping from what was painful.

This was Joachim's battleground where he suffered many wounds and years of pain, confusion, and frustration. He waged his holy war of good versus bad whether he engaged with his wife, his four daughters, his students, or his business partners. Joachim simply wouldn't deal with his discontent—or anyone else's. Emotions were the bad guy. He had to push them away. Spirit was the good guy. He had to court it and then hang on for dear life.

For Joachim, and most everyone, the unconscious mind perceives being human as the opposite of being divine—no matter what you believe consciously. Thus, it's impossible, logically, for you to be both simultaneously. But you can embrace both with your mystic's eye. Knowing you are both human (flawed) and divine (perfect) at the same time is the key to this different brand of happiness and a much more workable life.

When I introduced Joachim to the Six-Step Process, he was stunned. He saw how he had split himself in two and pitted one half against the other—divine versus human. Because he denied any value in emotional discontent, he was blind to its hidden wisdom. If he perceived something good about emotion, it was Spirit's light seeping through the dark. In disowning his human emotions and claiming his divinity, Joachim became arrogant and conceited. Given how much he believed in the "oneness of all things," he was pretty astonished at how he'd placed his emotions and humanness outside this whole Oneness—and he hadn't even realized it was happening.

After Joachim learned the Six-Step Process and gathered the wisdom of his discontent, his life went through a massive shift. He engaged in a more compassionate way with his wife, kids, students, and business partners. He discovered human emotion and divine light (fill in your own language here) are equally valuable—one is not better or less than the other. He discovered he could live with paradox, managing it instead of trying to get rid of it. And he could do that wherever paradox showed up, which was in a lot of places. He discovered the basic balance for being a happy human being is to be poised between magnificence and insignificance—with freedom to move between the two.

The Most Basic Life Balance

You need both magnificence and insignificance to steady and stabilize each other. Then you can move fluidly with the ups and downs of daily life.

The words of another modern Indian mystic, Sri Nisargadatta, point at a paradoxical truth.

MYSTICAL GUIDELINE #3

Love tells me I am everything.
Wisdom tells me I am nothing.

You know this truth intuitively, although you may never have considered it relevant to your happiness or peace of mind. When you're in love, don't you feel like you are everything? All the distinctions between you and your loved one seem to vanish. You're just alive, happy, and at peace with the deliciousness of the world. Ahhhh, love! Nothing can disturb you when you're in that state.

On the other hand, when you wake in the dead of night and find yourself gazing out the window, dumbfounded by the gazillions of stars before your eyes, it takes your breath away. In those moments, you know you're just a tiny drop of life in a mysterious universe—insignificant and nothing at all.

These two experiences are available to everyone—without exception. Nisargadatta goes on to say, "Between these two, my life flows." Have you ever entertained the prospect that your life flows between being everything and being nothing—back and forth, again and again? Most of us haven't. Nonetheless, it's a stunning and rather obvious possibility.

Instead, we believe our lives flow between fighting and making up, hating and loving, fearing and daring, loneliness and companionship, imprisonment and freedom, avoiding pain and clinging to pleasure, feeling like somebody and nobody at all.

In the next chapter, we'll explore this connection between opposites—how it affects you in your daily life, and just what Sengsten means when he talks about "the deep meaning of things." However, I warn you—it might seem a little X-rated at first, because opposites are really engaged in one hot and steamy love affair.

5

THE STEAMY LOVE AFFAIR
BETWEEN OPPOSITES

Max loved driving his Lexus. It was smooth and powerful—a fast way to get away. He saw the stoplight ahead turn yellow. He pressed his foot down on the gas and sped up to the corner, making a hard and fast right turn. His hands gripped the steering wheel while the car's wheels grabbed for the road. He felt a wonderful rush of power, strength, and daring. He was in control. That sense of momentarily merging with the car soothed his soul. As he straightened out the wheel, he felt the power and strength drain out of his body, replaced by an overwhelming wave of weakness. He was right where he was before—unhappy and frightened. A nasty voice in his head berated him: "You fool! Stop worrying. What if this stress starts affecting your speaking? What if your talks stop being in demand? You will fail!" Max turned up the volume of the radio until Mozart drowned out the ugly inner voice.

Max didn't have a clue how to handle his fear of failing. He didn't understand that his struggles and stress were directly connected to his desires for success, courage, and relaxation. He wasn't aware polar pairs operate as a happily married twosome, deeply in love, and they do it, paradoxically, *because* of the tension between them—not in spite of it.

What Max learned, and you'll learn here, too, is that each opposite in a polar pair has a role to play and a specific time to play it out. This changed his perception of that inner turmoil, and it will also help you change yours.

> When the deep meaning of things is not understood, the mind's essential peace is disturbed to no avail.

In the previous chapter, the mystic Sri Nisargadatta highlighted the "deep meaning of things" by pointing out that opposites flow between each other—back and forth—and then back again. Let's explore what this means in everyday terms—and why it's a good thing.

Your Inner Tug-of-War

Like Max, most of us want life to move in a straight line, from A to B. It doesn't. Life moves like a river streaming between its two banks, without antipathy or conflict. The river never says, "The right bank is better than the left bank. I'd better flow to the right and avoid the left." Similarly, our lives stream forward between pairs of polar opposites. Yet for us humans, there is a great deal of aversion and struggle.

Without awareness, your unconscious mind will consistently deem one of two options in a dilemma better (or safer) than the other: Trust is better than doubt. Acceptance is better than rejection. Closeness is better than distance. Or, doubt is safer than trust. Rejection is safer than acceptance. Distance is safer than closeness.

These polar opposites create the paradoxical dilemmas I talked about in the last chapter. They generate the familiar tug-of-war experience you feel in your body. You might verbalize it like this: "On the one hand, I trust you and think you're being truthful. On the other hand, I have doubts and think you're lying."

As you are debating in your mind about what choice to make, dilemmas are literally pulling you toward one choice and then the other, physically. As you go back and forth, you explore the pros and cons of each option, trying to decide which choice to make.

What Is the Deep Meaning of Things?

Like Max, you probably assume the turmoil you feel around opposites is something you're creating. It's something you should be able to stop and make go away.

Yet, here's the thing. You're not the one creating this turmoil. It is there by design to keep the flow of your life's energy both balanced and energized. It actually has nothing to do with you at all.

> *Opposites are complementary—not contradictory.*

You can make it worse—don't misunderstand me. But no matter how hard you try, you can't make it go away for good, never to return. Your turmoil has a specific job: to get your attention and move you—in that moment—in the most appropriate direction. Remember, discontent is life's messenger. When you gather its wisdom, you finally know your role in this process—and which choice to make.

The "deep meaning of things" can only be perceived when you understand that opposites are not fighting with each other at all. It looks and feels that way—I know. Nevertheless, what you see and feel is not hostile opposition.

Opposites Are in Secret Service

While your mind's eye perceives opposites in an antagonistic fight, your mystic's eye perceives them pursuing a different agenda. They are secretly serving your life's creative process. The push-pull you feel in your body—that inner tug-of-war between them—is nothing other than life's creative dynamic tension.

This dynamic tension has the job of keeping you stable and strong by continually re-balancing, re-energizing, and expanding your life energy. Life's creativity arises out of the dynamic tension between opposites. It forms the stage where you create your stories and play them out—whether they are tales of despair and redemption, or sorrow and joy.

Your mind's eye sees this tension as hostile conflict, but your mystic's eye sees it as harmonious discord. Both perspectives are needed. Together, they give your dual nature (divine and human) balance, clarity, and the wisdom to respond appropriately in each unique moment. This is the kind of paradoxical perspective mystics observe all the time.

Harmony in Discord?

At first, Max couldn't imagine harmony and discord in a cooperative alliance. He looked askance when I talked about relaxed tension.

I explained that in daily life, your mind's eye zeroes in on this tension as antagonistic discord. On the other hand, your mystic's eye perceives that discord as harmony. Both perceptions are happening simultaneously. As puzzling as it is, the "deep meaning of things" lies in understanding this paradox: your life is both harmony and discord—by design. It is both perfect and flawed—by design.

When you fully digest this nugget of truth about the human experience—you cannot have one without the other—you can keep a good sense of self-esteem and live your life with greater ease.

Opposites are not in opposition to each other.

When you greet life's tension as harmonious discord (or discordant harmony), your mystic's eye has awakened.

Puzzle Pieces Coming Together

Right now your way of seeing things probably doesn't match the mystics. The struggle to be right and not wrong can breed contempt and war—not peace. The fight to win and not lose can breed greed and deceit—not compassion.

You can't logically grasp polar pairs as harmonious because they are opposing experiences. It's not rational to say you're both right and wrong—both a winner and a loser. Yet your experience can be exactly that. Without any other way to make sense of it, your unconscious mind will feel confused, conflicted, and desperate to just pick one to end the extreme discomfort and fear.

Everything changes when you embrace your inner tugs-of-war as life's resourceful creativity in action. And guess what? It's rebalancing you so you can not only survive but also thrive!

The Risk-Loving Fireman and Security-Obsessed High School Counselor

Gillespie's nickname, Dizzy, fit him as perfectly as his profession. Dizzy was a thirty-five-year-old fireman with two other hazardous careers already under his belt—special ops marine and deep-sea diver. His hobby: skydiving. Clearly, Dizzy loved risk.

A simple philosophy drove his decisions: "Totality—in the moment! That's the best route to living out life's purpose and meaning with aliveness and gusto." Dizzy made this way of life sound so reasonable and wise you wanted to jump out of that little single-engine plane and dive into the open sky right beside him.

When he and his wife, thirty-three-year-old Angelina, came to see me, Dizzy was pursuing two more risky interests: commodity trading and real estate development (unfortunately this was during the 2008 worldwide recession).

Angelina was as obsessed with money, image, and security as Dizzy was with risky business. But her unconscious mind wanted her to love someone strong enough and forceful enough to ensure her security.

With embarrassment and chagrin, Angelina confessed her need for a macho man. She wasn't able to honor her own many professional achievements and accomplishments in her field of education. She didn't feel capable enough to create the security she longed for under her own power. She needed someone who could provide enough money to uphold her image (expensive clothes, etc.) and free her from the responsibility of caring for herself financially.

Angelina and Dizzy seemed to be genuinely in love. But their marriage was in crisis. After a few conversations, it was clear their conflicting attitudes toward money—both spending it and saving it—were the crux of the problem. When it came to making financial decisions, every conversation spiraled down into huge power struggles chock-full of manipulation, outright lying, and verbal fisticuffs. Trust had fallen on very rocky ground.

Learning the Six-Step Process taught Dizzy and Angelina how to understand and manage their differences. With this new wisdom, they built a financial plan for the future that balanced both Dizzy's need for risk and Angelina's need for safety.

They were shocked (and relieved) to discover they had each completely polarized to their own point of view. That meant Dizzy wanted risk 100 percent of the time and was closed to any of Angelina's "wimpy" choices for security, like CDs or a 401K. Angelina wanted security 100 percent of the time and was terrified by any of Dizzy's "irresponsible" choices involving risk, like investing in commodities or an Internet start-up company.

The Six-Step Process gave them a new way to relate to risk and security. For the first time they realized both were important considerations in all of their financial decisions. Their polarized views had blinded them to the value of the opposite opinion. Now they saw there were benefits to their partner's viewpoint—and there were weaknesses to their own.

Opposites are not in a fight. They are allies, not enemies.

Becoming aware of opposites—and how they work in a complementary fashion—freed them to flow between the two. I'm happy to say their marriage was saved—and they still use the Six-Step Process when any kind of power struggle starts to arise.

Check It Out for Yourself

Imagine how your life would be different if all the opposites you fight with—competition versus cooperation, close versus distant, trust versus doubt, praise versus criticism—were actually flowing between each other, without a fight.

Take a moment and explore your own experience. Don't impulsively believe what you're reading—or reject it. Check it out for yourself. If these words and polar pairs aren't relevant for you, substitute the ones that are.

- Does your work experience flow between success and failure?
- Do your friendships move between being easy to hard and then easy again?
- Does your faith move back and forth between trust and doubt, over and over?
- Does this movement between them happen many times in a day, or stretch out over weeks?

Your answers to these questions should show that these polar pairs are actually friendly fellows, and not mortal enemies—*if* you knew what to do with the tension you feel between them.

Complementary Contradictions

To just go with the flow can be hard to imagine. What are you going to do when that disliked opposite comes streaming through your body and mind, or into your life to deal with?

Another guideline from mystic psychology can help. On one of my trips to India, I was struggling with my dilemma around sitting still versus moving when meditating. I was attempting a lotus posture on a hard, cold marble floor while trying to listen to a discourse given by the mystic Osho. I was desperate to move and relieve the pain in my legs. But I also wanted to be respectful, which meant being still and quiet. Despite being in the throes of anxiety and near panic, I heard Osho articulate this perception.

MYSTICAL GUIDELINE # 4

Life is not made of contradictions.
It is made of complementary opposites.

I realized movement and stillness were complementary—old pals dancing to a rhythm I didn't yet know. Osho's words opened the door to a wiser way of approaching polar pairs.

Here are a few other complementary contradictions:

- Competition and cooperation are partners in the game of balancing your life.

- Acceptance and rejection are cohorts in expanding your personal growth.

- Rest and activity are allies in revitalizing your energy.

Awareness opens the door to seeing opposites in this new way.

Now consider this: What if these opposites are even more than old pals, cohorts, partners, and allies? What if they're caught up in such a hot and steamy love affair they can't ever leave each other's side?

The Steamy Love Affair Between Opposites

Polar pairs are complementary contradictions that not only don't fight each other, but also are passionate lovers. (If you've ever had a hot rendezvous, you know what I mean.) No matter how hard you try to separate them, their steamy love affair pulls them back together every time. They're irresistible to each other.

Remember Romeo and Juliet's story? Their love is so powerful that when Romeo mistakenly thinks Juliet is dead, he kills himself. Juliet, who hasn't really died, can't handle being without Romeo, so she kills herself as well—this time for real. A similar story unfolds for Tristan and Isolde.

This is the type of passionate love existing between our opposites—the kind that is truly, madly, and deeply fanatical. Opposites are actually incapable of leaving each other's side. (If you think of your partner as your other half—consciously or unconsciously—understanding this may generate some compassion for your own relationship troubles.)

The devotion of each experience to its polar opposite keeps them exquisitely interdependent. Each devotedly follows on the heels of the other, committed to being together forever.

The Interdependent Polar Pair

As a trainer of Ericksonian hypnosis and NLP, I teach the unconscious structure of language. In the world of conceptual reality (thinking), you can't conjure up one concept without your unconscious mind bringing up its opposite. You know how you feel love gives your life meaning? Polar opposites give each other their meaning. Try to define "good" without thinking of "bad," or "trust" without considering "doubt."

The mind and body define things through comparison. This is how you give a concept its meaning. Think "me" and the notion "you" will appear. They are an inseparable pair.

This explains why going after the good stuff and avoiding the bad stuff doesn't work for dealing with opposites. You may find the one you want and hold on for dear life. But you still can't banish the one you didn't choose. It strolls into your life, sooner or later, as an uninvited guest. For example, Max's work brought him outer success, but it also brought him inner failure since he couldn't hold on to his sense of happiness and achievement after he stepped offstage. Polar opposites always travel in pairs.

Check It Out for Yourself

Try to pull up the concept of peace without thinking about war. You'll find you can't. The notion of peace can only arise out of the notion of not having war. Without this notion at the unconscious level, peace has no meaning. Likewise, the idea of war can only arise out of the idea of not having peace. Without this idea at the unconscious level, war has no meaning.

Test out these other common opposites. If you pay attention, you'll become aware of what your own unconscious mind is doing:

- Can you entertain the concept of closeness without also thinking about distance?

- Can you contemplate the notion of being right without thinking about being wrong?

Opposites need each other to be what they are.

- Can you think about connection without calling up the experience of separation?

Let me put this unconscious pattern into words—and yes, you guessed it. It's a paradox. Polar opposites define themselves by the presence of the absence of the other. It defies logic, and it makes complete sense when you place that missing puzzle piece of paradox back on the table.

_____

Opposites are interdependent by definition.

_____

As you've just experienced, to think of peace, the concept of war is present, even when war itself isn't. To think of love, the concept of hate is present, even when hate itself isn't. Consequently, opposites are interdependent by definition.

So what does this mean? It's not your fault those unpleasant experiences—anger, rage, disappointment, frustration, anxiety, fear, failure, loss, or confusion—keep coming back. You're not doing it wrong. This is good news.

The bad news is that those unpleasant things are going to keep reappearing in your life—again and again.

Opposites Are the Fabric of Your Life

As I prepared for the weekend segment of one of my Whole Brain Wisdom School trainings, I overheard Deirdre, a lovely, well-respected fifty-year-old Irish marketing director in the hi-tech field, excitedly talking with other students. "This past month I just couldn't believe how many opposites and dilemmas I kept seeing. There are so many of them out there—every day! Everywhere! In practically every situation I'm in, I keep seeing opposites. I'm stunned that I've never been the least bit aware of this before." Others in the group began waving their hands and talking over each other as they shared having the same experience. I've seen this response over and over again.

Polar pairs are everywhere, and opposites are the fundamental fabric of your life. They're not just in your mind. They weave the unique patterns that make up your physical, mental, and emotional universe. A mere awareness of the idea starts to move your life from stress and anxiety toward peace and calm—simply by realizing how opposites permeate your days.

Here are just a few of the polar pairs floating around in the pool of life:

- Nature: wet/dry—height/depth—hot/cold—light /dark—small/big—barren/fertile
- Emotions: arrogant/humble—happy/sad—enthusiastic/apathetic—agony/ecstasy
- Relationships: parent/child—boss/employee—teacher/student—ally/enemy

Take a minute right now and make a list of all the opposites you can think of. If you can, ask a few other people to join you in this exploration. I think you'll be amazed how many there are that you've never thought of in this way.

A Fast Review to Digest Slowly

Let's do a quick review of what you've learned about opposites so far:

- Your unconscious mind is forced by your biology to navigate opposites—and the dilemmas they create—for maximum gain and minimum loss regarding your survival.
- Its only option is to move you toward what you want and away from what you don't want—grab the good, avoid the bad.
- This is not a great strategy for managing the flow of life because it creates dis-ease in your mind and body, leaving you feeling dissatisfied and discontent.
- Your mind's eye perceives the tension between opposites as antagonistic discord—a danger to your survival.

Now let's review what your mystic's eye can perceive when it takes a look:

- Opposites are complementary contradictions—not antagonistic enemies.

- There is creative dynamic tension between the two, no hostility.

- Opposites are interdependent. They cannot exist separately, because each defines itself by the absence of the other.

- Opposites are the fabric of your life. Once you start looking for them, I guarantee polar pairs will begin popping up everywhere.

Let's take your newfound wisdom about opposites and get even more specific about where and how the tenacious off-spring of their steamy love affair—those annoying dilemmas—show up in your everyday life.

6
DILEMMAS: OPPOSITES' TENACIOUS OFFSPRING

Maggie munched on her potato chips and sipped the new herbal tea, annoyed it was no longer steaming. She had to leave for Uganda the following morning, and the idea of traveling in the rain made her even more irritable. "I don't know if all this work to eradicate hunger and poverty is really making the world a better place," she mused. "I do love traveling, but I also want to stay home, cook up pots of pasta for friends, and write poetry as late as I want at night." She sighed and rested her head on the back of her chair. As if talking to the gods, she pleaded, "Couldn't I just stay home? Traveling isn't fun anymore. I'm always working—or recovering from working. Can't I have a personal life I don't have to squeeze in between trips and still try to save the world?" Dreading the inevitable stress of packing, she sluggishly pulled herself out of the chair; instead of heading for her suitcase, she wandered into the kitchen to try out that new coconut brownie recipe her friend described as "to die for."

Maggie struggled between two options: either commit to her professional life or commit to her personal life. Each time she chose one, the other reared its head. She thought choosing between them was the only way to save her sanity.

She couldn't opt for her personal life, because she needed to support herself. And she couldn't choose her business life because she had a husband, children, and friends who needed her (not to mention her private dream of being a writer). She had to participate in both. The stress of it all often made Maggie want to just give up and quit everything.

Some Things You Simply Can't Fix

Maggie was desperate to have her problems fixed. "I can't keep living with so much turmoil and pressure. This issue has to be resolved once and for all!"

It's totally understandable to want something to be fixed if it doesn't work—or to remove it if it gets in your way. But Maggie didn't realize that some things in life simply aren't fixable. She felt there had to be a right choice, and problems were always solvable. But they aren't. When the same dilemmas kept returning, the onus fell on her personal flaws. This depressed her deeply—over and over.

Do you believe all problems have a solution that will remove the problem permanently so you can move on? Remember—your mind's job is to find problems and create solutions. But you've already learned that the standard solution for fixing this kind of dilemma—setting up what you like against what you dislike—only creates more dis-ease in the mind and the body.

> There are some things in life you simply can't fix.

Two Kinds of Dilemma

Maggie wasn't aware of a small detail of monumental proportion: there are actually two kinds of dilemmas. One you can fix. The other you can't. And there are no personal flaws involved.

The Resolvable Kind

To be sure, there are resolvable dilemmas, where your choice between the two available options fixes the problem and it's over and done.

For example, say you're shopping for a new computer and you have narrowed it down to two models in your price range. Once you've chosen which one to buy, the problem is over—end of the dilemma. Or maybe you want to go out to lunch near the office and there are only two possible choices close by: a Thai restaurant and a burger joint. Once you've chosen, the lunch dilemma is finished.

The Unresolvable Kind

I call the second kind of dilemma an Unresolvable Dilemma. Remember that steamy love affair between opposites we covered in the last chapter? The polar pairs in an Unresolvable Dilemma can't ever separate permanently. This creates the predicament—there's no single decision you can make that will solve the problem forever; there's no clear or easy way out. Since this kind of dilemma won't go away, you can only learn to manage them. When you learn to do this successfully, the Unresolvable Dilemma loses its power to disturb you.

An Unresolvable Dilemma is like the mosquito that won't stop bugging you when you're trying to sleep. Living in a paradoxical world means Unresolvable Dilemmas will continue buzzing in your ear—again and again. If you want happiness and peace of mind, you'll want to know how to manage Unresolvable Dilemmas.

There are two kinds of dilemma: resolvable and unresolvable.

Common Everyday Unresolvable Dilemmas

Following are ten common Unresolvable Dilemmas. They were all a part of Maggie's life, and they are most likely a part of yours as well.

1. **Desire for action and desire for passivity.** For example, should you make the effort to hang up your clothes? Or can you just take a break and relax for awhile?

2. **Desire for connection and desire for separation.** For example, on the one hand, you want to be with friends tonight. But on the other hand, you're tired and would like some solitude.

3. **Desire to trust and desire to doubt.** For example, you have reservations about your abilities to succeed. Should you listen to them as truth, or should you question them?

4. **Desire to live a spiritual life and desire to live a comfortable material life.** For example, one part of you wants to go to a meditation retreat. But another part wants to remodel the kitchen.

5. **Desire to be part of a team and desire to be independent.** For example, should you put on that horrible shirt the bowling team voted to wear for team spirit, or should you be a rebellious individual by wearing a shirt that looks good on you?

6. **Desire for long-term gain and desire for short-term gain.** For example, you want to eat right and be healthy. On the other hand, you want to splurge.

7. **Desire to control and desire to surrender.** For example, you don't know whether you should take the lead over your project at work, or whether it's better to just follow your co-leader and do it his way.

8. **Desire to play it safe and desire to risk.** For example, you have to get home quickly. Should you speed up, or stay at the speed limit?

9. **Desire to be authentic and desire to be politic.** For example, on the one hand, you want to be honest with your boss—as well as your spouse and friends. But isn't being political the better choice?

10. **Desire to plan and desire to be spontaneous.** For example, should you plan out your entire day so you know exactly what to do every minute, or should you live in the moment, be spontaneous, and just let things unfold?

Where Do Your Dilemmas Live?

Dilemmas live in your everyday problems. In the Resources section, I've listed 149 examples of Unresolvable Dilemmas organized into the six most common categories where they appear:

- Relationship
- Power
- Success
- Happiness
- Purpose
- Faith

As you check out each section, notice if you experience conflict around any of the polar pairs—in either your inner or outer life. The ones that are demanding your attention will feel the most emotionally charged and mentally confusing.

Is Your Dilemma Unresolvable?

Here are four simple questions to help you determine whether your dilemma is resolvable or unresolvable—and thus must be managed. Think of a situation where you feel caught up in an either/or choice. Feel free to use the lists above (or in the Resources section) and change the content to fit your own circumstance. Then ask yourself these questions:

1. Can I feel the tug-of-war sensations in my body?
2. Are the two options I have to choose between polar opposites?
3. Does each opposite define itself by the absence of the other?

4. Does my problem go away if I choose either pole and ignore the other?

Answering yes to questions 1–3 and no to question 4 means your pair of polar opposites is interdependent and, thus, an Unresolvable Dilemma. Seeing this means you can stop trying to fix it and start managing it by using the Six-Step Process.

The Jazz Musician and the House Cleaner

Lorenzo and Jasmine had been married for one year. They had not lived together before they were married, and shortly after their honeymoon, trouble erupted. Four nights a week, Lorenzo played at jazz clubs. Six days a week he practiced with his group. Most of his time was spent with other people. When he came home, he wanted some alone time to compose music or just do his own thing without paying attention to anyone else's desires.

Jasmine worked six days a week as a housecleaner. She owned her own cleaning business, and when she wasn't cleaning, she took care of paperwork, managing who had paid, who still needed to be billed, and who was overdue. It was a work life of almost complete solitude. When she came home, she wanted company. She loved to share how her day was, chat, and go out to concerts, movies, and dinner with her husband.

As you might guess, their at-home time became the center of conflict. Lorenzo wanted to spend time alone. Jasmine wanted to spend time together. They tried every way they could think of to fix this clash between their needs—negotiation, compromise, complete surrender to the other's desire. But they both ended up feeling resentful toward the other person and unappreciated, unloved, and unhappy.

When I first explained to Jasmine and Lorenzo that they were right, this problem wasn't fixable, they looked shocked. They came to me for help, and I was confirming their worst fear: there was no way to fix the problem. When I explained there was a way to live with this problem and make it manageable, they each breathed a sigh of relief. Hope returned.

Lorenzo and Jasmine used the Six Steps to help them live with paradox, rather than struggling to banish it. They discovered there was wisdom in the natural flow between being alone and being together. Their at-home time ceased being a personal fight (an either/or predicament) and became a way to express their feelings of love and connection for themselves and for each other (a both/and adventure). What had been a confusing and distressing situation they had taken very personally became just a simple paradox of life that they could successfully manage.

Why Your Mind Gets Confused

Most people are perplexed at first, just like Lorenzo and Jasmine. Our unconscious mind will get confused around opposites, contradictions, and paradox. As you've learned, that's because it only has one option for dealing with them (grab one, avoid the other)—and it doesn't work.

Even mystical guidance can be confusing at first. Mystics agree contradictions and opposites do exist in life when seen through the mind's eye. They also agree that life actually has no contradictions and no opposites when seen through the mystic's eye. All is harmonious. And, paradoxically, both perceptions are valid.

Clarity begins when you realize our universe is built on the tension between polarities. However, the only place opposites appear antagonistic toward each other is in the mind. Your mystic's eye will always perceive opposites in harmony. It's a "Duet of One," as phrased by another modern mystic, Ramesh Balsekar.

Your Duet of One

You can find your own duet of one when you look through the special lens of paradox. Can you find evidence of a battle at dusk as the darkness of night takes over from the light of the day? Can you find any problem when dawn slips in and frees the darkness to take a sabbatical for a while? Day even invites darkness to hang around in shadows and shade. And night reciprocates, requesting the stars and moon to share their luminosity. Is there anything going on but a seamless transition from one to the other?

Outside the human mind, there is no antagonism and no problem with the flow between opposites. The remainder of this book is a navigational guide to finding this seamless flow. Understanding you have a mind's eye and a mystic's eye makes you ready to enter the Land of Unresolvable Dilemma. Remember that invisible bridge from the Introduction? Now you're going to learn how to make it appear right before your eyes.

7

ENTERING THE LAND OF
UNRESOLVABLE DILEMMA

Max pulled up to the Center for Global Public Relations. In thirty minutes he'd flip his inner switch and step on stage, stoked and ready to address an assembly of educators with his keynote speech. He turned off the radio and reached inside his suit coat for some nicotine gum—his mojo for remaining a nonsmoker. He grabbed his briefcase and climbed out of the car. Giving the car door a strong slam shut, he muttered, "You think you can keep this up forever? Someday someone is going to discover you're a fraud and don't know a thing about being happy. You've got a good pitch, but we both know you're really a loser." No matter what Max tried to do with this hateful voice—ignore it or fight with it—it left him exhausted. Now he'd have to hit the men's room to pull himself back together. Disgusted, he threw back his shoulders and walked into the building—as if he really were the guy they all expected him to be.

Without understanding he was dealing with an Unresolvable Dilemma, Max was at the mercy of his emotions and his inner critic. When he learned about paradox, he got terribly excited. He thought his problems would be solved: he would never again have to fear failure, his inner critic would be silenced, and happiness and peace would start permeating every moment of his day!

Life in the Land of Unresolvable Dilemma

Oh, if that could be true! But that's not the reality in the Land of Unresolvable Dilemma. You're not being offered one side of life that seems better than its opposite. Like Max, you learn the knack

You're learning the knack for living peacefully with both sides of life.

for living peacefully with both sides of life—divine and human, light and dark, high and low, winning and losing, succeeding and failing, loving and hating, order and chaos, happiness and sorrow.

The wisdom of your discontent guides you to live peacefully with life as it is—even as you strive to make it different. And it leads you to an oasis of inner peace that remains undisturbed by the presence of your emotional turmoil, and life's flow between opposites.

This is only possible when you put the missing puzzle piece of paradox in place. This kind of inner peace is real—and reachable. The happiness it brings easily invites unhappiness in for tea. Wow! Imagine you can allow what makes you unhappy into your picture of a happy life. That has to be a magical land, doesn't it?

Home of the Happiness That Knows No Opposite

Anytime you navigate two levels of reality (in our case, human and divine) at the same time, it is magic. Like any good magic, your mind can't fathom how it's done. But when the rabbit pops out of the hat, you're amazed by it anyway.

Your mind may get a little confused by this notion, but give it a try anyway. This different brand of happiness knows no opposite because it embraces all opposites equally—happiness and sadness, pleasure and pain, gain and loss, connection and separation, birth and death. It's bigger than any set of polarities, and it accepts everything as part of the harmony of all things.

This happiness exists in the realm beyond thoughts and ideas; it lives outside the territory of the mind—beyond the world of conceptual thought. And this place is, literally, just a blink away from your mind's eye.

You already know this place in times of quiet when you're just being (like when you're sunbathing, lying on the massage table, or soaking in the tub) or during noisy, fast, and dangerous times when you must be present for your safety (like when you're white-water rafting, skiing, surfing a big wave, or mountain climbing). In these scenarios, your mind naturally becomes quiet—and that different brand of happiness arises. This is why we like these kinds of activities. When the mind is still—even for just a tiny bit of time—you connect directly with your life experience (that's you minus your story).

Have you ever stood at the ocean's edge in the middle of a winter storm, mesmerized by its power and beauty? Have you sensed a majestic harmony, even though waves are crashing all around, and huge piles of heavy driftwood are shifting, rearranging the contour of the shore? Just being with the power of nature feels good, and a sense of happiness and peace arises.

This happiness is not the mind's idea of happiness—getting what you want and not getting what you don't want. Instead, it's just being with what is unfolding. Deepak Chopra once said that happiness arises when you don't resist the continual flow of events. What you may not realize is that includes embracing your resistance to not resisting. It's such an odd thing to do . . . until you do it.

Mystics perceive each moment of life for just what it is—pleasurable, painful, or neutral. This perspective can be yours when you know how to live with paradox and how to navigate opposites, which simply means using your mystic's eye.

Suspending Your Disbelief

Your imagination is the key to suspending your disbelief and finding the Land of Unresolvable Dilemma. Without it, you may never find the inner peace that knows no disturbance and the happiness that knows no opposite.

If your skeptic has appeared, as mine always does, you may feel cynical. Hang in there. When you give your imagination an inch, it will happily take you a mile. Follow your inner knowing that there is a different brand of happiness—and imagine you're hot on its trail.

Imagination helps your brain move out of old patterns into this new view of your world, preparing you for travel through the Six-Step Process.

How to Make the Invisible Bridge to the Land of Unresolvable Dilemma Appear

The reason you may not see the bridge leading to the Land of Unresolvable Dilemma is because it's blanketed by heavy mists. This fog is created by your discomfort related to opposites, and it blocks your mystic's eye from seeing what's there. When you see through the haze of ordinary understanding of opposites to the clarity of mystical understanding on the other side, you can locate the Land of Unresolvable Dilemma.

Take a moment right now and dream up a fantasy—a faraway place surrounded by mist and fog. Imagine you suspend your disbelief in mystical lands and magical happenings. Place any doubt, skepticism, or cynicism—all of which are normal—on a shelf just at the back of your mind. (Don't worry. It will still be there if you want it back.)

To get the mists to lift, consider the notion that opposites are complementary and interdependent—friends, not enemies. Conjure up two polar opposites, like acceptance and rejection, in a loving embrace, dancing together in an intricate, yet simple routine you've not seen before. Open your mind and heart to the possibility that opposites might not be fighting with each other. Imagine the mists are lifting.

To get the fog to dissipate, pretend you can hear a strange music arising in the distance, with a harmony unfamiliar to your ears. Fancy this harmonious discord is emerging from a loving duet played by cooperation and competition, alone and together, or love and hate, as they exhibit their complementary and interdependent nature. Envision the fog dissipating.

Then imagine with your whole being—as if it is really true—that the swinging footbridge comes into view. Watch the pathway open, as if by magic, and then you're ready to cross over the chasm below.

How to Cross the Bridge

This bridge will take you from struggling with either/or predicaments to the wisdom of your discontent just on the other side—and that map for how to relax with life as a both/and adventure.

You can see the bridge is made of rope—very sturdy yet flexible rope. Every step on the footbridge is made of this rope—there are no boards. And each rope step is in the shape of an infinity loop—that ancient symbol representing the eternal flow of life's energy back and forth between polar pairs.

Now all you have to do is walk across it. But even thinking about it feels intimidating. You might even reconsider, deciding that getting to the other side is not so important after all. To mitigate your fear, you talk to someone who's crossed it before. Crossing the bridge would feel a lot safer and be a lot easier if you—okay—knew the ropes.

The Three-Point Balancing Act

Based on knowledge from the mystics, I'm going to show you the easiest, most efficient, and safest way to cross the bridge—and live with paradox. I call it the Three-Point Balancing Act. It keeps your mind and body grounded in your human life where your mind's eye focuses on the conflicting desires in a world of opposites while simultaneously keeping your mystic's eye focused on the spiritual view of opposites' harmonious nature.

The Three-Point Balancing Act allows you to access two different levels of your reality, making each immediately available to the other, and to you. You can finally make sense of that enormously confusing dilemma of being both human and divine at the same time.

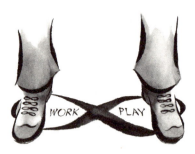

First, place your right foot on the outside edge of the loop on your right (see picture above) and your left foot on the outside edge of the loop on your left. Then place your body so it is balancing in the middle just above where the two sides of the infinity loop cross.

Imagine your mystic's eye is awake, open wide, and taking in the entire dynamic unfolding directly beneath your feet.

What does it feel like to stand on both sides of the infinity loop, and both sides of a polar pair, at the same time?

This solid stance keeps your feet grounded, connecting you to your experience of the flow between opposites—your human life. Then your body-mind can better ride the waves of endless movement between opposites—and it keeps you filled with the sensations of aliveness.

Meanwhile, the clarity of your mystic's eye, by virtue of seeing a larger view, perceives the complementariness, interdependence, and harmony between the two sides of the polar pair—and the eternal rebalancing their dance provides. It keeps you connected to your spiritual life, and filled with a peace that remains undisturbed by the endless flow of change your body-mind must undergo every day.

Let's take a look at how using this Three-Point Balancing Act impacted another of my students.

The Image Hound

Nick was street-smart, business savvy, and a snazzy dresser. A performer at heart, he compulsively wanted attention. He loved nothing better than raving accolades for his achievements. It made him forget, momentarily, that he was the ruined alcoholic he knew himself to be.

Nick was a thirty-five-year-old lawyer who worked for five years for an international health organization specializing in international law. Every month he traveled to Africa to encourage and educate governing bodies how to better legislate issues of health and wellness.

You can't escape having both a dark side and a light side.

Despite all the good he did, Nick didn't know what was important to him. He cared about his wife and daughter more than he cared about saving Africa or the world. And he felt terrible because he was still sneaking drinks when he traveled.

When Nick told me he used to be a "mean, motorcycle-riding, gun-toting son of a bitch," it was hard to believe. In my office, Nick was one of the sweetest and smartest guys I'd met. But he was angry about being an addict. So he focused on the outer life of success and accomplishment instead of his inner hell of rage, self-hatred, and his daily urge to damn it all and go drink.

After he got the hang of using the Three-Point Balancing Act, things changed for the better. Nick found a spiritual context for his life that changed how he felt about everything. He relaxed into the discrepancy between his outer and inner worlds because he now saw a larger picture that embraced his being both an alcoholic and a Marketplace Mystic.

Some days, Nick says he's still rude and self-focused. Other days, he's kind and helpful. Either way, he generally feels okay and loveable every day, regardless. "Before, I couldn't find myself. I was constantly running away from my pain and toward any kind of pleasurable escape. Realizing there's a higher partnership between what I thought were polar opposites changed everything. I'm not so angry anymore with myself or with others. I'm maybe even a bit more open with my heart—and that really feels good."

Nick has been sober now for over four years. He discovered he liked helping people one-on-one. He gave up traveling to stay home with his wife and daughter, found a new job where he still excels, and practices being present to the days of his life. He reports, "My days are filled with more joy and peace—even when I'm feeling miserable and angry. It's an amazing relief."

The Beginning of Your Both/And Adventure

Once you cross the bridge and step into the Land of Unresolvable Dilemma, like Nick, you can discover with great joy that your life is fundamentally a both/and adventure; you can relax and feel a huge wave of relief.

You understand you can't get away from being human, and you can't get away from being divine. No matter how far you transcend, no matter how much you transform, no matter what you learn or understand about life.

Your body-mind will always feel the effect of this steamy love affair between polar pairs, but you know now that it's not your fault. It's by design.

The Three-Point Balancing Act lays claim to both your divinity and your humanity as relevant and essential. It creates a new channel of connection, communication, and communion between your material life and your spiritual life.

If you want to integrate your spiritual life more fully into your human life, learn to embrace the unalterable fact of your dual nature. It's a paradox. It is the key.

The next chapter brings us to perhaps the most crucial notion for peaceful traveling through the Land of Unresolvable Dilemma. You're going to take a fresh look at the magical side of perhaps the most important yet disliked, denigrated, and ignored part of reality—and that is impermanence, or change.

If you want to be a happier and more loving person, help your body-mind feel at ease with also feeling unhappy and hateful. It's a paradox. It is the key.

8

THE MAGIC OF IMPERMANENCE

Maggie awoke to a lead-like sensation in her stomach. It was undoubtedly that half pan of brownies she'd consumed the night before. Their sugary energy helped her pack for her trip, even though it still took half the night. Ignoring her nausea, she stretched the kinks out of her body, rolled out of bed, and pulled on her usual traveling clothes. Sadly, her time at home was over, and she was off to work once again. First she was home, then gone, then home again, then gone again. How could she find any balance in life if she couldn't catch her breath? When Maggie did have time to herself, it went by so fast she usually missed it. A flood of sadness and anger engulfed her. It seemed no matter what she thought or did, she failed at making her life what she wanted it to be—happy, productive, and peaceful. With a heavy sigh, she glanced at the clock, grabbed her suitcase, and ran out the door to catch her plane—late once again!

With so much traveling under her belt, Maggie—I assumed—would be comfortable with change. I was wrong. When I mentioned impermanence, she blurted out, "I hate it." With vehemence, she continued, "I get where I'm going, and then I have to worry about what's happening back home or back at the Hunger Project I just left. Everything changes while I'm gone, and I get exhausted trying to keep up—which I can never do anyway."

Few people greet change with a cheery "Welcome!"—although for some, change can squelch boredom and make life interesting. Most folks find a modicum of change delightful—a new kind of salad dressing on the dinner table, a surprise refund check from the government, a new hairstyle. But big changes—like losing your job, buying a house, moving to a new city, unexpectedly becoming pregnant, or losing a spouse or close friend—can be distressing and frightening. No matter where you go or what you do, change comes with you. Even the monk meditating on a mountain deals with change: a stomach virus, a flood washing away the temple, the arrival of a chatty novice.

This chapter talks about the value of making impermanence your adviser by becoming more aware of its presence and the vital part it plays in your daily life—including its essential role in the hot topic of manifestation.

I've never talked to anyone who didn't agree, at least grudgingly, that everything changes. Here's a guideline credited to the ancient Greek mystic Heraclitus:

MYSTICAL GUIDELINE #5

The only thing permanent is impermanence.

You know it's true. Still, we remain optimistic that we can make some things permanent, whether it's our bank account balance or our happiness. It's a peculiar human behavior. Despite all the changes we experience every day—from the weather and the stock market to moods and thoughts—the unconscious mind still believes change is dangerous. (It's that survival thing again.) Your unconscious drives you to try to make things stable, secure, and—yes—permanent.

Continual change creates quite a dilemma. We like change because we don't want to be bored. For example, one night we enjoy chicken enchiladas, another we delight in chicken curry. On the other hand, we don't like change because it makes things unfamiliar and insecure. For example, when you travel you want a new adventure, differences, a shift in your daily routine. But you don't want too much change. (Please let there be a toilet!)

You will always be affected by these two paradoxical desires. The dilemma of impermanence will be your traveling companion for life, and it makes a powerful case for learning how to let go. Well, how exactly do you do that?

The Six Steps will help you release both compulsive holding on to the past and compulsive planning for the future—while you simultaneously learn from the past and explore your possibilities for the future. Then life is brighter, softer, calmer, and sweeter—as if all the sounds of existence gather and improvise a symphonic celebration in your honor.

Fearing Change

Let's check out Heraclitus again. Even though he died in 475 BC, some things, paradoxically, never change.

MYSTICAL GUIDELINE #6

You cannot step in the same river twice,
For other waters are continually flowing in.

Sitting on the bank of a river, you realize different water is always flowing by. Put your hand in the stream. Feel its movement streaming through your fingers. Change is a natural, everyday occurrence.

Yet we work hard to make things last as long as possible— whether it's a relationship, job, car, or bowl of ice cream. Do you ever say to yourself, "I should have been able to make things stay the way I wanted them to"? Even with all our efforts, we can't succeed. Change inevitably comes.

Most of us fear the change of death as a permanent bad change that removes what you love—your grandma, dad, partner, friend, or beloved pet. We think the opposite of death is life.

One spring morning in India, my guru was talking about living without fear. As I sat in that huge, marble-floored tent surrounded by towering bamboo and fragrant flowers, he pointed out the opposite of death was not life, but birth.

I was so astonished I lost awareness of my pain from that hideous lotus posture. I realized that life flows *through* birth and death. It's life that connects each to the other. Seem obvious? Yet fear makes this connection easy to miss.

The whole premise behind religion and spiritual paths is that life continues on after death. That makes a good case for rebirth and reincarnation. But whether you consciously believe in reincarnation or not, the unconscious belief that death is the final end to life can skew your willingness to go with the flow. Why? Because it sets the stage for your unconscious mind to ignore or deny the reality of change.

> The opposite of death is not life, but birth.

It's a powerful unconscious belief. It not only generates fear but also blinds you to the magical side of impermanence: the miracle of creativity.

The Magical Side of Impermanence

Impermanence creates growth—have you ever noticed that? Without change, the seed couldn't crack open for the seedling. It would have to stay a seed forever. Without change, the heart couldn't crack open for the emergence of love. It would have to stay guarded forever.

Even death plays a powerful role in the creation of life—in all its forms. Mystical psychology (which differs from ordinary psychology) operates with the notion that death is not the end of life.

Life uses birth and death (and other opposites) to create its journey. Physical death is only the end of a part of life—the journey that enjoys exploring in human, animal, or botanical form. For us, it is the end of experience as we currently know it, on this plane of reality.

Life is nothing but change—literally happening right before your eyes—moment to moment. When you disregard, overlook, deny, or refute the reality of change, you miss the flow of life. The problem arises when you try to control change—and that's exactly what your unconscious mind wants you to do. It says no to change because it's risky—and it values safety more.

But we want both safety and risk. We control because we're convinced we're missing something, and we want it. But are we really missing anything? Have you ever tried to contemplate the here and now at a precise point in time? If not, give it a try this minute. In the actual moment, it's hard to find anything that's missing. You'll find that you have to admit everything is fine—unless your mind's eye is showing you stories about what's unfolding—making it good or bad.

Our stories always include some interpretation of the moment: horribly wrong, wonderfully right, sadly missing, or gratefully present. Seeing this with your own eyes is (sorry about this) quite an eye opener.

Life is really nothing but change.

Inside your mind, life is troublesome when risky, and safe when secure. Outside your mind, there's no story and no comparison. There are just the facts—"what is." Curiously, that makes life's intrinsic beauty very obvious.

The I-Want-to-Be-Perfect Personal-Growth Junkie

Tess was a sixty-year-old hi-tech head hunter passionate about improving herself. As much as she wanted to change, it scared her unconscious mind. She was a longtime student trained in every personal-growth process since 1972 (I'm not kidding)—and her unconscious mind resisted all of it.

After working with the Six Steps, she developed a powerful yes to change. She presented me with two gorgeous Waterford wine glasses, etched with a yin-yang symbol on each side and a card that said, "My friend, these glasses are already broken. Please enjoy."

Embracing impermanence deeply touched Tess's life. She shared the following: "Once I got this impermanence thing, everything changed. When I bought my new car, I heard myself whisper, 'It's already dented.' When I got my new sunglasses, I said out loud, 'They're already scratched!' And when I bought my new set of hand-painted Italian dinnerware that brings me so much pleasure every time I take a plate or cup out of the cupboard, I quietly cried and tearfully said, 'It's already chipped.'"

These kinds of reminders didn't stop Tess from buying what she loved (or going to self-improvement courses). They simply kept her present, grateful, and free to enjoy them while they were here.

All things must change from what they are into something else. Ignoring this means missing powerful guidance from life. Sooner or later, whatever you have will no longer be there. You'll reach for it and find nothing but thin air. Remembering that change will knock on your door makes life juicier—and you freer to enjoy each moment as it arrives and departs.

This Too Shall Pass

When you consciously remember this moment's pain will not last forever, patience arises. Happily, you know the pain will end. When you consciously remember this moment's pleasure will not last forever, compassion arises. Sadly, you know the pleasure will end, too. Whatever the content of your moment, just say, "This too shall pass."

Learn to embrace change and navigate opposites.

Inner peace arises when you can navigate what is undeniably true about life—impermanence and opposites. These two facticities shape your life. How you respond to them shapes your response to life.

Embracing impermanence allows you to find the flow of life. Knowing how to navigate opposites allows you to go with that flow.

Check It Out for Yourself

Let's review what you can verify for yourself. Please, *don't* believe me or take what you're reading as truth. The only way to change information into knowledge and knowledge into *your* personal wisdom and skill is to really consider these questions for yourself.

- Change is a daily reality. Agree or disagree?
- Life moves back and forth between opposite poles. True or not true—according to you?
- All polar opposites are interdependent because each defines itself by the absence of the other. Accurate or not?
- Opposites are a matched pair, working in a complementary fashion, to create a harmonizing balance between them. Certain of this, or not sure yet?

Using the Six Steps will help you determine where and when these things are happening in your daily life. The permanence of change and the complementary nature of opposites are connected and fit together in a particular fashion. Let's see exactly what that is.

> *Embracing impermanence allows you to find the flow of life. Knowing how to navigate opposites allows you to go with that flow.*

The Permanence of Change and Opposites

The flow of life can't happen without the permanence of change. Change allows the unending flow between opposites—back and forth, and back again. Life flows from the strengths of one opposite to its own weaknesses, then to the strengths of the other side and its own weaknesses—forming a pattern just like an infinity loop.

For instance, with "together" and "alone," you move from the connection you feel with others (strength) to overstimulation (weakness) to the self-direction of being alone (strength) to loneliness (weakness) and back to the connection with others.

> *The home of unresolvable Dilemma is the flow of change itself.*

You can verify all you've been reading about when you simply look, with fresh eyes, inside the flow of change.

Developing this new skill is like walking into a dark movie theatre. At first, you can't see anything. You blink a couple of times, wait a minute so your eyes can adjust to the different level of light, and then you can see what's there—seats, an aisle, and a screen. It's a natural phenomenon. Your eyes are built for it.

Your brain is also built with a natural ability to see opposites using that mystic's eye that is naturally yours. Give yourself a minute to adjust to the notion and then take a look at something changing in your life—like your job, relationship, exercise routine, or living situation.

All the things you discovered about opposites will begin to show up right there, inside the flow of change: the movement back and forth between polar pairs, their interdependence, and their complementariness. Be patient, stay focused, and look with your mystic's eye.

Now let's shift the focus of your mystic's eye to the tricky challenge of manifestation. What does impermanence have to do with creating your own reality?

The Flow of Change and Manifestation

The constant flow of change also affects how you view the past, decide in the present, and anticipate the future. Is the future out of your hands? Or is there something you can do today to secure it?

One of the most confounding Unresolvable Dilemmas lives in the context called manifestation, made popular by the book and movie *The Secret*. According to the Law of Attraction, you can manifest what you desire. First, you identify what you want, then you imagine it already being the case—see it, hear it, and, most importantly, feel it as if it's already here as your current reality; stay completely positive in your thinking and speech, then let it go. Don't *hope* it will happen; *expect* it to have already happened; know it!

Manifestation requires both making things happen and letting things happen.

Visualization and a bit of time-shifting are required, but the directions for manifesting are straightforward and accurate. So why do so many people following these guidelines fail to manifest what they want?

Simply, these directions are only half of the truth about manifestation. It's not just about making things happen as you want them to. There's another side to the coin, the polar opposite—letting things happen as they want to. Together they create a polar pair, and each plays an important role.

Most people think the Law of Attraction operates according to the following limiting belief: You, as personality, are enough to get you what you want. Just desire it, see it, and feel it, and it is yours. You alone create your own reality.

It's easy to fall into the grips of the opposite limiting belief, too: God, Spirit, or the Divine has total control over your life; what will come will come, and you have no say; karma is king, and what you're going to get is what you've already put out there—sometime, somewhere, in some life. God alone (via the creation of karma) creates your reality.

Is it possible to make things happen and also let things happen, to be active and passive?

- To actively create your future—make things happen—follow the directions I noted above.

- To actively allow your future to unfold—let things happen—follow the directions to meditate, stay in the now, be present to what is, and go with the flow.

If you're unaware that manifestation is an Unresolvable Dilemma you have to manage, it's easy to split yourself apart. You feel you have to make a decision to either focus your attention on your material life, or your spiritual life.

But what you really want is the best of both worlds. The key is being aware of this crucial polar pair, and the central role of impermanence, the ebb and flow

> There is an ebb and flow between making things happen and letting things happen.

between making things happen and letting things happen. Imagine they are interdependent and complementary. Imagine there is harmony in that discordant tug-of-war you feel in your body.

To balance these two seemingly contradictory viewpoints—making things happen versus letting things happen—do the following:

1. Recognize them as an interdependent polar pair.

2. Embrace them as the flow of life moves back and forth between them.

3. Watch each one arise and pass away in your body-mind.

4. With your mystic's eye, see them as complementary and deeply in love.

5. And, most important, notice which action is being requested of you moment to moment. Is it time to focus your attention and imagine the future as you want it? Or is it time to let go of the future and let it unfold as it will?

When the gardener is planting his garden, he engages in making things happen. Then, knowing the nature of how things grow, he lets things happen. Nature takes over. The seeds follow their own blueprint, unfolding in their own design to bring the bounty and beauty of the garden to fruition. The gardener does only what he needs to do: water, fertilize, and weed.

Manifesting is about balancing the polarity of control and surrender. It's balancing the involvement of your personality and the involvement of your Spirit in the creation of your life's journey—my will versus Thy Will.

Knowing how to live with paradox, opposites, and impermanence is essential to manifestation. It is particularly relevant in manifesting peace of mind on a daily basis—that different and life-changing brand of happiness. Using the Six-Step Process, you can learn precisely how to both make it happen and let it happen, allowing this balancing to emerge.

> There is a happiness that knows no opposite. You have to both make it happen and let it happen.

The Security of Insecurity

None of us ever know for certain what is going to come next. Not knowing what the future holds can make life an adventure, or it can be a mighty good reason to stay cloistered and minimize risk. Whether you feel insecure around change or you embrace it, change is greatly influenced by how you navigate this root dilemma: you want things to stay the same so you can feel secure, versus you want things to change so you can feel alive.

How do you manage these contradictory desires? You might struggle, become confused and frustrated, and end up feeling numb or paralyzed if you don't know these two reactions to change are complementary and interdependent.

Within this mess of uncertainty, unpredictability, and insecurity, there is a pattern to guide us. It rests inside the flow of change.

- Knowing how to go with the flow, be here now, and live with presence creates a paradoxical security in the face of life's insecurity.
- Relaxing with the fact you can't control the future creates a paradoxical certainty in the face of life's uncertainty.
- Even though you can't predict what's going to happen, there's a paradoxical predictability in knowing it will soon be the opposite of what's happening now.

Your Life: Balancing in Motion

Being present to impermanence is the magical ingredient for creating balance in your daily life—whether you're concerned about your health, finances, partnership, parenting, job, career, family, or spirituality.

Although we think of balance as a place to get to, it is not actually a destination. Why? It is a verb, which is a process. Unresolvable Dilemmas are the epitome of this balancing in motion. You can go with the flow between

There is a pattern to guide us through life's continual change. It rests inside the flow of change.

complementary polar opposites most easily when you are aware of their continual rebalancing and can accept their complementary nature.

Have you ever tried to stand completely still, with no movement at all, allowing not a hint of movement in your belly or chest when you breathe, and not a sway of your body side to side or front to back? It's impossible. Trying to create complete stillness calls forth greater movement, and sooner or later you lose your balance. The balance between stillness and movement is essential to your body's stability.

Grabbing for the good and avoiding the bad, running toward success and away from failure, or demanding silence in your meditation and condemning the noisy inner dialogue sets up the same kind of interference. In the presence of a polar pair, unconsciously taking sides creates imbalance. In the extreme, it creates polarization and, potentially, a complete lack of movement. For example, the issues of abortion and the death penalty in America are so clouded with controversy between people who support opposing poles that it's nearly impossible for public policy to be decided. The dialogue has become completely defunct.

Balancing is life's method for creating harmony. Your life is continual balancing in motion: steadiness requires wobbling, and stability requires wavering. It takes getting used to, but once you know wobbling and wavering don't mean you're a bad person—or in danger—it's a great relief. You can actually begin to relax.

Unresolvable Dilemmas are balancing in motion.

Real Harmony

Are you beginning to see why setting up what you like against what you dislike makes no sense? You can't stop the process of rebalancing, no matter what you do. It is the natural harmony of life. And you can't stop your unconscious mind from trying to survive.

So, what to do? How do you realign with the natural harmony of things? Another mystic friend, Ta Hui, says:

Real harmony is neither to go with nor to go against.
Instead, let reality possess you.

Ta Hui is talking about the reality of opposites, which you can verify for yourself:

- Opposites are the fabric of your daily life.
- Opposites continuously flow between each other, in a complementary and interdependent fashion.
- Inner tugs-of-war in your body are that flow.
- The wisdom of your discontent tells you which way is the best way to go in this moment.

You can code this wisdom into your brain and body—just like the mystics. Wouldn't it change the way you meet the flow of everyday life?

Balance is a process—not a place.

The If-I-Don't-Do-It, It-Won't-Get-Done Executive Director

Lou was a forty-five-year-old workaholic not-so-happily embroiled in his life's passion—a non-profit for the performing arts. As the executive director, his agenda of to-do items wouldn't quit. He spent twelve hours a day at the office, and then a few more working at home at night.

His need to be 100 percent responsible for everything kept him smoking and overeating. This kept him going until he dropped; then he'd push a little further, creating more exhaustion and worry. Unfortunately, the notion of shared responsibility was beyond Lou's comprehension.

When he came to see me, Lou's health was at risk, his anxiety was out of control, and he had only a semblance of a personal life left. "Everything is out of balance," Lou complained. "But I can't shake my need to be responsible—not even for a minute. I know

I can't do everything I'm supposed to get done, but I can't stop trying!'

A little voice in his head kept saying, "What you're doing with your life is so selfish, childish, and without purpose. You have to excel to redeem yourself." Despite this nagging feeling, Lou's first words to me when we met were, "I don't do 'inner.' I thought you should know." You can imagine his inner struggle.

However, when Lou discovered work and play went together like wet and dry, or up and down, his face lit up like a Christmas tree. It was amazing to watch. I saw his mystic's eye open as he clearly saw, for the first time, that he didn't have to choose one over the other. His professional life and his home life were an inseparable and loving twosome, and when left to their own rhythm, they naturally balanced each other out. Intellectually, he'd known both were valuable; but emotionally, only work got the kudos. Now he could also relish play.

Most importantly, Lou learned that work and play, responsibility and freedom were just experiences for him to explore—

Real harmony is neither to go with nor to go against.

and not defining statements about his value and worth. "My daily life works so much better. I don't get disturbed by unfinished projects now, and I even stay calm when I can't make gnarly decisions quickly."

No one can rid themselves completely of their personality or conditioning. You just make your peace with them being what they are—your personality and conditioning. They are not *who* you are. This brings us to our next mystical guideline, again from Ta Hui:

MYSTICAL GUIDELINE #8

Allow that which is inescapable to overwhelm you
and you will find immense peace.

The reality of opposites is inescapable; it's the basic pattern in our daily lives, and the phenomenon that produces conflict, tension, ambiguity, and contradiction.

But your mystic's eye gives you the freedom to stop fighting and start embracing the wisdom of your discontent. The wisdom of your discontent tells you the following:

- Peace arises when you perceive opposites as an organic unity.

- Polar pairs are the two sides of the same coin—and that coin is Oneness, or the Whole.

- Your mystic's eye can perceive this Oneness hiding out inside the flow between opposites.

You can't change the fact of gravity, and you can't change the fact that opposites are inseparable—no matter how long you fight it, or how hard you try.

Yes, you can transcend opposites. But that's not the same as seeing through them with your mystic's eye. When you keep your feet on that infinity loop, grounded in the life of your body-mind, you can claim both dimensions of your being; you can honor the reality of your human self with the guidance and support it needs from your divine self for a peaceful journey.

Giving your unconscious mind *the option to be neither for opposites nor against them* is the key to a new deeper relaxation for your body—even though, paradoxically, you'll still take positions. And the body's relaxation is the key for your mind's new understanding to take root and blossom.

Now it's time to move on to chapter 9, where you'll gather the final items you need to pack for an enjoyable and comfortable journey through the Land of Unresolvable Dilemma.

> Relaxation is the key to understanding. Understanding is the key to relaxation.

9

PREPARING FOR YOUR
PEACEFUL JOURNEY

*Max heard the applause and saw the audience rise for a standing ova-
tion. This was the best part of his career, making the rest tolerable. He
had achieved his goal—giving a good talk and inspiring his audience.
As he strode off stage, many of the participants crowded up to the edge,
reaching out to shake his hand and say thank you. Max felt happy.
There was no questioning his success—the proof was all around him.
But as the crowd thinned out, the joy and strength he so enjoyed began
fading, like air was seeping out of his balloon. Crushed that this hollow
feeling had again been waiting for him, he sat down on a stone bench
just outside the building in a lovely courtyard complete with fountain
and stone labyrinth. On a whim, he got up and began to walk on the
labyrinth toward the center. He wondered if staying focused on the path
would lessen his anxiety and help him find a solution to his problems.*

As skeptical as Max thought he was, he was actually quite an ex-
plorer of different pathways to success. Though he didn't know it
yet, he was about to walk a new path—one that showed him how
he could live with failing—and still be happy and successful. By
learning the Six-Step Process, Max learned to notice what happened in his own body every time he felt caught between his two
opposing options—success or failure.

This chapter helps you pack for your journey through the Land of Unresolvable Dilemma. You've already shaken up your ideas around opposites, impermanence, and paradox. All you need now is a few more tools. The good news is that you already have them. You won't need all of them all the time, but it's nice to have the items packed in your bag in case the need arises.

The Tools You Need

1. **Curiosity:** They say curiosity killed the cat, but not in this case. Instead, curiosity gives more life to your day. Since you already know how to be curious (even if it's only about the latest gossip at work, or your friend's date last night), you're just going to shift what you get curious about. The object of your curiosity is now going to be your inner tug-of-war. Curiosity will help you notice what that tug-of-war feels like in your body and mind—the pull in two different directions, the urge to make a decision, the movement back and forth between the two choices, like putting your foot on the gas and then on the brake—back and forth again and again. The key is to get a little nosy. Pay attention to your tug-of-war feelings, rather than getting anxious or zoning out.

2. **Conscious awareness:** Conscious awareness means paying attention on purpose to whatever you're doing or to whatever is happening to you. To experience it right now, place your attention on different parts of your body: your left foot, the tip of your nose, the back of your neck where it meets your clothing, the sensation where your hand is resting right now. As you purposefully move your attention around your body, you're paying attention on purpose. When you're confronted with the stress of an inner tug-of-war, combine your curiosity with conscious awareness. This powerful duo will get you new information about what's really going on.

3. **Intention:** You use your intention every day. You intend to get up. You intend to make breakfast. You intend to have a cup of tea or coffee, get dressed, and brush your teeth. This

just means you're directing the focus of your conscious attention. Now I didn't say you were consciously aware of every bite of food, or every sip of your steaming morning eye-opener, or every swipe of your toothbrush. While that would be nice, the point is that you already have the tool of intention and are using it every day. You just want to combine your intention with your curiosity and conscious awareness. This means you *intend* to focus on learning how to embrace polar pairs rather than seeing one as good and the other as bad. Then you will travel through what feels like an inner war zone with less stress and anxiety, open to noticing what you didn't see before.

4. **Willingness:** To get the most out of using these tools (curiosity, conscious awareness, and intention) you want to be willing to have a pleasant and fruitful journey. How do you have willingness when part of you resists? You already know the answer—paradox, of course! You can be both resistant and willing at the same time. For instance, you're willing to get up and go to work even though you're resisting going out of the house. Or you're willing to drive your friend to the airport even though you're resisting the idea of getting into the car yet again. Coming up in Part Two is the way to help bolster this willingness. Then the real adventure begins—navigating life's contradictions and feeling inner peace at the same time!

5. **Imagination:** To find your way to the land where inner peace and calm are king and queen, you have to imagine as if it's actually possible. You've used this tool a few times already in earlier chapters. Even if you don't believe you can visualize, haven't you, at some time, fantasized a different life, a better body, a more caring partner, or a more successful career? You know how to imagine things. All you have to do is suspend your learned disbelief in the possibility of peace of mind and a different brand of happiness. How? Take any skepticism, cynicism, or fear and imagine as if you could put it in the coat closet just at the entryway to your mind. If you need

your disbelief back, don't worry. It will be right where you left it.

6. **Conviction:** Everyone carries convictions (or sacred beliefs). Some convictions allow expansion, while others set limitations. Either way, you have this necessary tool for creating a peaceful journey through your inner conflicts. Setting out on this paradox exploration is like swimming upstream. This kind of practical wisdom is not yet conventional wisdom, so you're probably going to run into a lot of flak (self- and other-generated) about what you're trying to do. It was your decision to begin looking for another way, so trust your own experience, inner knowing, and guidance from your heart and soul. Being convinced this exploration is right for you will make your journey easier.

7. **Doubt:** Here's another paradox: Are you certain enough of your newfound way of thinking to question it along the way? Is your conviction that you're moving in the right direction strong enough to allow you to also be unsure? Doubt is the essential tool to balance your convictions and keep them fresh. Conviction by itself is both necessary and dangerous. Still another paradox! Doubt allows you to remain open to the possibility your conviction may not be 100 percent accurate. Maybe you don't know all you think you know: consider the possibility that your convictions may be based on unproven or faulty information. Doubt helps you remain open to expanding your perceptions. You welcome and explore new knowledge and new pathways to peace.

8. **Connection to something larger than yourself:** Having a sense of connection to something larger than yourself is tremendously helpful. It doesn't matter whether you call that something God, Goddess, Mystery, Nature, Universe, Buddha Nature, your Essence, Christ Consciousness, Suchness, the Tao, the Dharma, or any other name. And it doesn't matter whether that sense of connection is real or imagined. It's great if you can actually feel a connection to something

larger than yourself, but if you can't, don't worry. Just imagine as if you could.

TOOLS YOU NEED:

Curiosity	Imagination
Conscious Awareness	Conviction
Intention	Doubt
Willingness	Connection

Acknowledge cynicism, but don't let it stop your personal exploration. Imagine as if the world were a friendly place, as if God (Universe or Mystery) were friendly and wanted you to be happy, peaceful, and to live a life filled with love. It might be a stretch, but it pays off to give it a try. As a lifelong cynic, I can vouch for how powerful this tool can be in changing your journey through the day from misery and negativity to joy and gratitude.

Starting the Adventure

Now that you have these eight tools consciously in hand, and the mystical perspective on opposites, dilemmas, and impermanence from the previous chapters, you're about ready to start navigating that inner tug-of-war in a new way. Remember, our mystic friends have already demonstrated how to do it; you're just going to follow in their footsteps.

Having the tools you need, you will easily move through the six specific steps. These steps show you the following:

- A new route to peace of mind in the presence of emotional turmoil
- The ease of living in a world of paradox
- A different and life-changing brand of happiness

One note of caution: Be aware of the Awareness Paradox. Awareness can be your best friend and ally. It can also be your worst enemy. Why? Because your unconscious mind believes that once you're aware *of* something, you *know* it—and therefore can live it in your behavior. Unfortunately, this is hardly ever the case.

The first effect of increasing your awareness of impermanence and opposites will be a decrease in your felt need to read on and learn how to change your behavior accordingly.

This is exactly the opposite of the desired outcome. The goal of this book is to give you six steps that can actually change your brain, and thus your behavior, in the presence of continual change and your emotional turmoil around it. So remember: understanding the notion of impermanence is radically different from embracing the reality of impermanence.

To set up what you like against what you dislike is the dis-ease of the mind.

Now you're ready for Part Two, where you'll again meet up with both Maggie and Max. Along with me, they will be your traveling companions through the Land of Unresolvable Dilemma.

You'll focus with Maggie as she learns how to embrace and balance both her personal life and her professional life. And with Max, you'll concentrate on how he discovers his ability to embrace and manage his desire to remain successful and his growing fear of failure. This would be a good time to take a moment and consider one Unresolvable Dilemma in your own life that you'd like to understand and learn how to better manage. There are lots of examples of Unresolvable Dilemmas in the Resources section, but the Six Steps are best learned by staying focused on one dilemma at a time.

Let's begin.

PART TWO
YOUR MAP TO THE LAND OF UNRESOLVABLE DILEMMA AND THAT DIFFERENT BRAND OF HAPPINESS

The resistance to the unpleasant situation is the root of suffering.
—RAM DASS

You know quite well, deep within you, that there is only a single magic, a single power, a single salvation . . . and that is called loving. Well then, love your suffering. Do not resist it, do not flee from it. . . . It is only your aversion to it that hurts, nothing else.
—HERMANN HESSE

10

BEYOND THE
AWARENESS PARADOX

Congratulations! Reaching into Part Two means you've successfully navigated your first challenge—the Awareness Paradox I talked about in the last chapter. Your willingness to keep exploring the Six-Step Process means you're receptive and open (despite any skepticism), and you're ready to take your imagination out for a good long walk. In Part One, you successfully dreamed up a compelling vision of the swinging footbridge to the Land of Unresolvable Dilemma. You took a look through the lens of paradox and saw the unusual Three-Point Balancing Act between two dimensions—an essential for living with, and managing, paradox. You're all set to go.

You're going to walk through each of the Six Steps four times—once with Maggie, once with Max, once with my prime dilemma (which turns out to be an issue for a lot of folks), and finally, with your own dilemma. Each step has a different angle and will help install the process into your brain.

The Essential Element for Success—
Changing Your Brain

If you want to get results and awaken your mystic's eye, working through one of your own dilemmas is extremely helpful. This Six-Step Process is not only practical but also brain changing.

Your brain can make the change you want—and apply it to your life. Your active participation accelerates your brain's ability to install this new option of embracing opposites.

Do we need speed here? It's questionable whether we have years to accomplish this shift in human awareness through conversation, therapy, and meditation alone. The legacy of our mystic friends is this Six-Step Process—a koan in modern form gleaned directly from the psychology of the mystics. (A koan is a Zen Buddhist riddle of sorts. Its goal is to throw you outside the realm of thinking logically so you can directly experience the reality of something beyond the mind.) The Six Steps attempt to mirror this pattern of brain activity common to mystics.

The Wonder of Neuroplasticity

Remember chapter 8 on impermanence? Everything, including your brain, changes. Your brain actually generates new neural pathways, or coding, that affect its functioning. This little piece of magic now has a fancy name: neuroplasticity.[7] Neuroplasticity fashions new neuron trails by adding or removing neural connections, or adding cells. Pretty amazing, isn't it? The best part is that it means you can indeed teach an old dog new tricks.

Current scientific theory suggests that thinking, learning, and acting actually change both the brain's physical structure and functional organization. As you think and learn about Unresolvable Dilemma and, most importantly, *act in a new way by using the Six-Step Process*, you speed up your brain's ability to adapt.

Both mystics and neuroscience say your brain is already hard-wired for seeing opposites in this new way. Your mystic's eye is already there, just as real as your physical eyes, but dormant. Stimulating your brain with paradoxical thinking awakens your mystic's eye. Thousands of folks who have used the Six-Step Process report the desired new behaviors do begin appearing.

As you read on, use your imagination again. Conjure up the possibility of new brain cells lighting up. Envision new neural pathways popping into view as you learn how to embrace both sides of a polar pair and to perceive it as one unified whole.

Imagine watching and feeling a new option arise—the opportunity to view life as an adventure through the lens of *both/and* (your mystic's eye) rather than viewing it as a predicament through the lens of *either/or* (your mind's eye).

Reading and doing the Six-Step Process stimulates your brain. It will transform the wisdom of your discontent into your own wisdom, freeing the new behaviors you desire to emerge.

Your Travel Companions: Maggie and Max

You've already gotten a glimpse of Maggie and Max in Part One, but let me fill you in on their back stories.

Maggie

Maggie was raised in a fundamentalist family on the Eastern Seaboard of the United States. When she realized that her family's lifestyle was not to her liking, she left home, got married, had a child, and then divorced. As a single mom on welfare, she put herself through college and then law school, and she went on to dedicate her life to helping others—particularly focusing on alleviating poverty and hunger and on bettering the status of women around the world. She became quite well-known for her work in the field and was asked to consult with many international organizations who wanted her expertise.

When I met her, she was the mother of two children and had married a loving man. Together they made enough money to be upper-middle-class Americans living a beautiful and comfortable lifestyle. Several of Maggie's close friends were avid spiritual seekers. As she watched her friends grow and change, she envied their calm and centered way of being. She began longing for some kind of spiritual nourishment of her own. Maggie hoped that would be possible for her, but she couldn't get her head around the paths her friends were following.

Maggie's cynicism and fear of looking foolish were the overriding roadblocks to her exploration. But her courage and longing were stronger. She wanted something to give her life more meaning.

When I met Maggie, she was discouraged with her work, feeling it wasn't making much of a difference in the world. She wanted to stop traveling, stay home, and fulfill her dream of becoming a writer—and she wanted to write about her experiences abroad and all that she'd learned. She thought that might be a better way to help change the world, but she didn't know how to accomplish the task or fulfill her dream. The focus of her time with me was her desire to change her life and to send it in a more balanced direction.

Max

Max was born and raised in a tiny log cabin in Alaska. His father taught him all the things you had to learn to live in Alaska (fishing, hunting, hiking, chopping wood, staying warm in the cold), and Max discovered he loved working with his hands. He was always building something—and enjoying it immensely. At the same time, he knew there was more to life. There was a lot of wealth and glamour out there in the world, and he wanted some of it.

He studied hard and got his degree in architecture. But life took him in a different direction, and he found himself pulled into big corporations where his skills as a manager and speaker were fostered and rewarded. Max got a taste of the good life and went after it at full speed. Success became his most important goal. Although he had a lovely wife and four children, Max stayed focused on his career—with the aim of gathering as many executive perks as he could.

After several years and lots of promotions, Max quit his job as an executive vice president in the building industry and quickly established himself as a public speaker. He loved being on stage and receiving recognition for his achievements, but he didn't love anything else about it.

When I met him, his fear of failure had mushroomed to monumental proportions. He felt stalked by the threat of defeat. Because Max had always been a closet personal-growth junkie, he knew a lot about self-help. But this time, he needed more personalized support. Our coaching work focused on helping him learn a new strategy for managing his escalating fear of failure and managing his obsession with success.

Despite his stage persona, Max was actually shy and very sweet. He wanted some clarity and specific guidance for how to stop worrying about failure and to just enjoy his life, and he wanted to stop being so afraid of emotions—others' and his own. He saw them as a weakness rather than a strength, and he avoided even acknowledging them as much as possible.

In doing the Six-Step Process, Maggie and Max voiced a lot of objections that reflected the concerns I've heard over the years as I've taught this process around the world. I've included them all here to help you as you work your way through the Six-Step Process too. If you have any concerns that aren't answered here, just let me know (*www.RaginiMichaels.com*). The input of people like you has helped this work grow into a precise and effective tool.

Now, on to Step One.

11
STEP ONE—EXPLORING THE LAY OF THE LAND

TOOLS YOU'LL NEED FOR STEP ONE:

*Your **imagination** and **conscious awareness:***
to see the map of where you're headed.
(These tools will be useful in all the steps.)

Step One shows you how to map out the lay of the land that is your Unresolvable Dilemma. To navigate this predicament, you use the infinity loop to represent the terrain in the Land of Unresolvable Dilemma. Remember, the infinity loop symbolizes what is never ending—in this case, the flow between opposites—from here to there, from this to that and back again. In Step One you identify the landmarks that help you determine your location in this new territory, moment to moment.

Where Are Your Dilemmas?

You will find your dilemmas are actually your everyday problems. That's why your brain needs to know the specific situation or circumstance in which you want to explore opposites. This information increases the brain's effectiveness in giving you what you want.

Tell yourself (your brain) that in a certain setting, you now want to *move away* from either grabbing for the good or avoiding the bad. Instead, you want to move *toward* embracing both sides of the polarity in play, perceiving it as one inseparable whole.

Ask yourself, Does my dilemma show up in my intimate relationships, my work life, my friendships, my finances, my spiritual life, my emotional life? Be as specific as you can. (For help, check out the Resources section or chapter 6.)

Identifying the situation and its context is an important first step. If your conflict is whether to speak up and tell your spouse when you're angry or to hold your tongue to keep the peace, the context is your intimate relationship. But the way you act on your temper can change completely if the context is your work life and you're irked with your boss. You can have the same issue in lots of different situations, but the appropriate way to deal with that issue can change depending on the context.

HERE'S WHAT WE'RE GOING TO DO IN STEP ONE:

1. Map the dilemma: Start charting your map for the Land of Unresolvable Dilemma by drawing an infinity loop and identifying the situation.
2. Ask: Can we fix it?
3. Verify: Is the polar pair interdependent, and thus an Unresolvable Dilemma?
4. Identify: Write your perception of the strengths and weaknesses of each pole on your infinity loop map.

Alerting Your Brain with a Box

Identify where your dilemma (or predicament) appears, then write it above the infinity loop in a box like the one on the facing page. This alerts your brain to where the Unresolvable Dilemma you're working with plays out, and thus, where to make the change you're requesting.

Maggie

Maggie felt pulled between her desire to fill the demands of her professional life and her desire to fill the demands of her personal life. She wrote *Needs of My Professional and Personal Life* in the box. She soon discovered that her professional life meant work and her personal life meant family. There was, in fact, no space or time for acknowledging her needs and desires beyond pleasing others.

Max

Max wrote *Achievement* in his box. This goal preoccupied his days (and nights). Like accumulated dust, it covered everything he did with a layer of stress—work and family activities alike. It dominated his perception of every situation and had become the purpose of his life. Every task was a challenge to either succeed or fail—whether the goal was generating international acclaim or loading the dishwasher efficiently.

Ragini

Above my infinity loop, I wrote *Faith*. This was my stickiest issue. If I let my heart take the lead and gave in to trusting, I felt vulnerable and at risk. If I followed my mind's input and let doubt take the lead, I felt safe and protected but also that I was missing life. This predicament still accompanies every decision I make. It runs through my life like an underground stream. In my younger years, it was the playing field for stress, anxiety, and fear. Finding the Six-Step Process taught me how to calmly accept and manage its recurring presence in my daily life.

You

Now it's your turn. Grab a piece of paper (butcher size is the best but smaller will do fine) and draw your own infinity loop—and make sure you include a box above it. What will you write in the box? This is the first step in mapping out the lay of the land of your own Unresolvable Dilemma. Choose the predicament you want to explore and identify where it shows up in your life. Write that in the box above your loop.

Polar Pairs

Next, take time to find the polar pair at the root of the problem. It's easier to find the right set of polar opposites involved in your inner tug-of-war if you think in terms of opposites. See the Resources section for more tips on developing this skill. Attending one of my Facticity trainings (see *www.RaginiMichaels.com*) will also help you develop your capacity to find your root polar pairs. Trainings also emphasize awareness of presuppositions, which is a great help in identifying polar pairs and Unresolvable Dilemmas.

We'll ask specific questions to draw out the answers we need to move forward. Let's look at Maggie's dilemma first.

Maggie's Map: Self or Other?

Maggie came to me thinking that the problem was her job. It took up too much of her time. After some exploration, she realized she never felt like she had time. It didn't matter whether she was traveling, working at the office, or at home. When she wasn't consumed with saving the world, her time quickly filled with taking care of family and friends. The core issue wasn't her professional life versus her personal life. It was whether to fill other people's needs (clients and family and friends), or to fill her need for solitude, writing time, and reflection.

Her dilemma: whether to take care of other peoples' needs or her own. It was a gnarly either/or predicament causing Maggie distress and persistent emotional turmoil.

The Six Steps helped her relax in the presence of the continually recurring demand to fill everyone's needs, including her own.

Can She Fix It?

There are two kinds of dilemmas, remember? If your problem can be permanently fixed by choosing one option over the other, you can bypass the Six-Step Process. The Six Steps only apply to Unresolvable Dilemmas—the ones that keep returning, again and again.

Maggie was pretty sure this was unresolvable. She described it this way: "It's not like a coat I can just shrug off and throw away. It's more like a second skin—I can't go anywhere without it coming along with me."

Is It Interdependent?

To make certain the dilemma was unresolvable, Maggie checked to see if the polar pair was truly interdependent.

Remember chapter 5 and the steamy love affair between opposites? In an Unresolvable Dilemma, each opposite must define itself by the absence of the other to qualify as mutually dependent.

When this criterion isn't filled, you run into problems. You must be certain your polar pair is actually a polarity. For example, desire and fear do not create an interdependent polar pair because they don't define themselves by the absence of the other. You must find the opposites at the root of the issue. See the lists of interdependent polar pairs in the Resources section to help you.

In Maggie's case, her root polar pair turned out to be self and other—in the context of satisfying needs. She explored the issue. *Self* didn't have any meaning without the notion of *other*, and *other* didn't have any meaning without the notion of *self*. It was the same for the concept of *me*—it had no significance without the concept of *you*. These notions can't stand on their own because they are inseparable and interdependent. Maggie concluded her dilemma was definitely unresolvable. She couldn't fix it. She could only learn to manage it.

When a polar pair is interdependent, you can't conceive of one without thinking of the other. They are inseparable.

Once you're certain the dilemma is unresolvable, map out the polar pair on your infinity loop by placing the name of each pole inside one of the loops, like so:

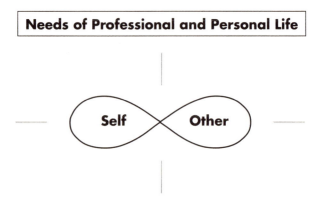

Maggie had part of the lay of the land mapped out. She knew where the dilemma appeared—in the circumstance of fulfilling needs. She knew what polar opposites were at play—self versus other. And she knew the dilemma was unresolvable. But more detail was needed to complete the map.

Opposites Have Strengths *and* Weaknesses

When you're struggling with a dilemma, there are always landmarks that you immediately recognize. They're like road signs that let you know where you are and your options for where to go next. To complete her map, Maggie had to identify the significant landmarks she knew she'd find.

She saw these markers as either pleasant things to cling to or unpleasant things to avoid. Her emotional reactions colored the landscape. Maggie wasn't yet aware that her landmarks were actually the strengths and weaknesses that naturally accompany each side of a polarity.

Strengths of Fulfilling Others' Needs

Strengths are like benefits—they feel good and are pleasurable. As Maggie listed the benefits of attending to the needs of others in her professional life and home life, she wrote them out above the part of the loop holding the word *Other*, I asked her to simply write the ideas that came to her, without holding anything back or worrying about the format of the list. Here's Maggie's list:

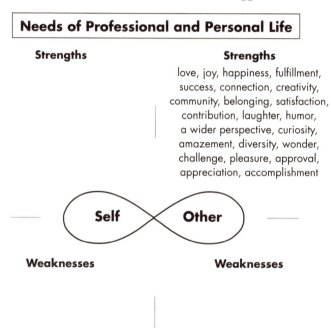

Needs of Professional and Personal Life

Strengths

Strengths

love, joy, happiness, fulfillment, success, connection, creativity, community, belonging, satisfaction, contribution, laughter, humor, a wider perspective, curiosity, amazement, diversity, wonder, challenge, pleasure, approval, appreciation, accomplishment

Self ✕ **Other**

Weaknesses

Weaknesses

She had lots more, but I suggested that was enough for now. We switched focus to the weaknesses of this behavior.

Weaknesses of Fulfilling Others' Needs

Weaknesses are like liabilities—they feel unpleasant and can make you feel vulnerable. I asked what happened when she filled the needs of others *to the degree that she neglected her own*. She wrote them out under the bottom of the *Other* loop:

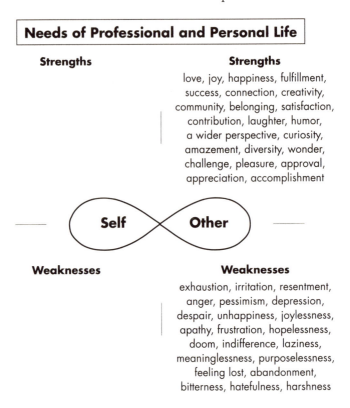

Needs of Professional and Personal Life

Strengths   **Strengths**
love, joy, happiness, fulfillment,
success, connection, creativity,
community, belonging, satisfaction,
contribution, laughter, humor,
a wider perspective, curiosity,
amazement, diversity, wonder,
challenge, pleasure, approval,
appreciation, accomplishment

Self   **Other**

Weaknesses   **Weaknesses**
exhaustion, irritation, resentment,
anger, pessimism, depression,
despair, unhappiness, joylessness,
apathy, frustration, hopelessness,
doom, indifference, laziness,
meaninglessness, purposelessness,
feeling lost, abandonment,
bitterness, hatefulness, harshness

Strengths of Fulfilling Her Own Needs

Then Maggie and I looked at the other side of the polar pair—*Self*. I asked Maggie about the strengths of paying attention to fulfilling her own needs. At first, she said, "I have no idea. I haven't done it in so long, I can't think of anything."

Maggie began realizing she was polarized to helping others. This meant she was committed to the rightness of pleasing others and had determined that pleasing herself was wrong. Her unconscious mind had set up the act of pleasing others as better than pleasing herself.

Without her awareness, her unconscious mind moved her toward fulfilling other people's needs and vigorously away from fulfilling her own needs. She reported this accurately described her life—outer and inner. She wouldn't even interrupt a conversation to fill her own need to go to the bathroom or to quench her thirst.

I asked Maggie to imagine as if she could have time to fill a few of her own needs. If that could happen, what kind of benefits or strengths would it bring her? She came up with these:

Needs of Professional and Personal Life

Strengths

happiness, creativity, fulfillment, satisfaction, joy, meaning, purpose, sense of belonging, connection, optimism, drive, single-mindedness, vision, insight, motivation, self-acceptance, participation in life, gratitude, recognition, pleasure, time for reflection, awareness

Strengths

love, joy, happiness, fulfillment, success, connection, creativity, community, belonging, satisfaction, contribution, laughter, humor, a wider perspective, curiosity, amazement, diversity, wonder, challenge, pleasure, approval, appreciation, accomplishment

Self   **Other**

Weaknesses

Weaknesses

exhaustion, irritation, resentment, anger, pessimism, depression, despair, unhappiness, joylessness, apathy, frustration, hopelessness, doom, indifference, laziness, meaninglessness, purposelessness, feeling lost, abandonment, bitterness, hatefulness, harshness

When she thought about it (which she wouldn't normally let herself do), Maggie *did* know what she was missing by not attending to her own needs. This is what made the dilemma difficult. She wanted others to be happy, and she also wanted to be happy herself; two seemingly conflicting desires demanded her attention. She didn't walk around consciously focused on what was missing, but she knew unconsciously. The two desires kept tugging at her heart and demanding gratification.

Weaknesses of Fulfilling Her Own Needs

I asked Maggie what might happen if she did pay attention to her needs to the degree that she *neglected* others (her clients, friends, and family). This time there was no hesitation. She knew exactly what would happen:

Needs of Professional and Personal Life

Strengths

happiness, creativity, fulfillment, satisfaction, joy, meaning, purpose, sense of belonging, connection, optimism, drive, single-mindedness, vision, insight, motivation, self-acceptance, participation in life, gratitude, recognition, pleasure, time for reflection, awareness

Strengths

love, joy, happiness, fulfillment, success, connection, creativity, community, belonging, satisfaction, contribution, laughter, humor, a wider perspective, curiosity, amazement, diversity, wonder, challenge, pleasure, approval, appreciation, accomplishment

Self **Other**

Weaknesses

guilt, selfishness, hell, isolation, greed, huge ego, narcissism, self-importance, self-indulgence, arrogance, cockiness, egotism, haughtiness, being too big for your britches, pride, overconfidence, being a bad person, ugliness, cruelty, unkindness, unfriendliness

Weaknesses

exhaustion, irritation, resentment, anger, pessimism, depression, despair, unhappiness, joylessness, apathy, frustration, hopelessness, doom, indifference, laziness, meaninglessness, purposelessness, feeling lost, abandonment, bitterness, hatefulness, harshness

As Maggie completed mapping out the lay of this land, she grasped what she'd previously been unable to sort out. Each pole brought her both pleasant and unpleasant experiences. She saw exactly what she wanted—and what she wanted to avoid. Her confusion got clearer.

That completes Step One for Maggie.

Max's Map: Success or Failure?

Max's core dilemma was success versus failure. But it wasn't just at work. It spilled over into his personal life as well. He was terrified of failing his wife, kids, and friends; he didn't have a clue what to do with people when they got all emotional. Inside, he felt unhappy, trapped, and deeply alone—a painful situation for a man with such a loving heart. At work, he described himself as more machine than man; and at home, more cash cow than beloved husband and father.

As you follow Max through the Six Steps, you'll see how he came to manage both success and failure at work and at home. Max learned how to live with the continual flow between the two. He discovered how to manage his fear of failure (and of other people's emotions) rather than being terrorized by an unavoidable life experience.

He had already placed the word *Achievement* in the box above his loop. Now he wrote *Success* and *Failure* inside the two loops, choosing where he felt each one belonged.

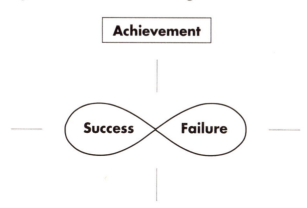

Can He Fix It?

Max hoped and prayed this dilemma was fixable. He wanted it to go away so he could be happy and successful—and finally relax. This dilemma had been Max's sidekick for over twenty-five years. Because he believed the problem was fixable, he always felt like a failure when it kept showing up, again and again. The failure he was trying to avoid kept nipping at his heels.

I pointed out to Max that success and failure were involved in an eternal love affair. One simply could not go on without the other. He didn't like the idea. He thought this meant he would fail to the same extent he succeeded. He voiced his hope that this notion was wrong. I told him that failure could happen in various ways—like not being able to train his dog to heel, or not completing a marathon. Failure didn't have to happen just to his income or reputation. But his fear of failing was threatening his career, so he agreed to check out the idea and use the formula for identifying an Unresolvable Dilemma.

In an Unresolvable Dilemma, each pole defines itself by the absence of its opposite.

If this dilemma really couldn't be fixed to the point it would permanently disappear, Max needed to face that—as a fact—before he could proceed. That meant confronting his skepticism that his problem would ever change.

Is It Interdependent?

Max's habit was to race past any hint of failure as quickly as possible. I asked him to slow down a little, take a breath, and contemplate, for a bit longer than a New York minute, whether or not success defined itself by the absence of failure. He chuckled and agreed to give it a try.

He settled back in his chair, closed his eyes, and for about ten minutes, seriously contemplated the notion of success. He concluded, "I can't make any sense of success without thinking of failure. I tried to think of failure without thinking of success, and I couldn't do it. I guess you're right. As concepts, they're inseparable." Seeing this clearly, Max felt stunned, and a little sad. With success and failure inseparable, there was no way to get rid of the problem permanently. They relied on each other for their identity and were thus interdependent.

Max operated under the same slightly crazy unconscious belief most people have: avoiding what you don't want will bring you what you do want by default. His revelations made him both relieved and uncertain. He realized he could stop trying to fix it because he'd never succeed, but he wasn't sure what to do next. He said, "Okay, but what do I do now? I see your point, but I'm still all bound up inside."

Although his quandary couldn't be eliminated for good, I assured him there was a way to handle it. Here comes the Six-Step Process to the rescue!

Strengths of Success

Max had no problem listing the strengths or benefits that came to him when he successfully achieved his goals. He wrote them above the loop holding the word *Success.*

Obviously, Max had good reason to cling to success. It brought him everything he valued.

Weaknesses of Success

I asked Max to put his attention on the weaknesses that also came with success. I directed him to imagine putting all his attention on success—to the exclusion of any focus on failure. He said, "I can't think of any downside to success. In fact, the key to success is to stay focused on it and avoid thinking about failure."

I reminded Max of his earlier discovery—that success and failure were inseparable and interdependent. He sighed, took a deep breath, and said, "I know. I can see that intellectually. But emotionally, I can't get there. And even if I could, I don't have a clue what to do with that information."

It was important for Max come to his own conclusion—to find his own way. So I suggested we leave the space under the bottom of the Success loop blank for a while as we moved on.

Max's inability to find any downside to success gave me a clue. He was living under the influence of *polarity blindness*. Polarity blindness is a complete polarization (attachment) to one side of a polar pair. Choosing that side becomes the best and *only* acceptable choice. You can recognize polarity blindness when you see only the benefits of the pole you cling to (no weaknesses) and you see only the weaknesses of the pole you avoid (no benefits).

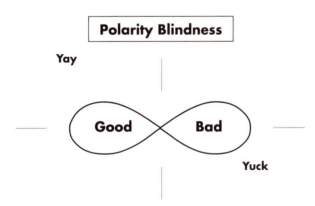

This means there's no awareness of the dance between opposites—no consciousness of their harmony or complementary nature. In fact, even mentioning these ideas evokes strong opposition.

Strengths of Failure

To test my hypothesis about Max's polarity blindness, I shifted his attention to the loop with *Failure* written in it. I asked him to write down the strengths, or benefits, that came to him via this experience. With conviction, he said, "There aren't any benefits here. Failure isn't an option. It's the end of everything. It's an obvious weakness with no strength anywhere!"

My hypothesis proved true. Polarity blindness was at work. We left that area blank as well and moved on to the weaknesses of failure.

Weaknesses of Failure

In a snap, Max completely filled up the area under the bottom of the *Failure* loop.

Achievement

Strengths

achievement, praise, recognition, accolades, appreciation, wealth, happiness, enjoyment, satisfaction, self-esteem, pride, accomplishment, approval, love, respect, attention, kindness, colleagues, triumph, name recognition, fulfillment, contentment, gratitude, acknowledgment

Strengths

Success **Failure**

Weaknesses

Weaknesses

being a loser, a dud, a has-been, unworthy, nameless, faceless, invisible, and lost; blame; embarrassment; poverty; anonymity; shame; humiliation; mortification; chagrin; fear; terror; anger; rage; self-pity; self-hatred; dread; anxiety; frustration; guilt; sadness

No further questioning was needed. Max was blind to his own polarization toward success and away from failure. He was incapable of seeing the weaknesses of his own highest value. And, he couldn't see any benefits to what he was most afraid of.

Intellectually, Max knew this couldn't be true. He expressed willingness to look a little deeper. I sent him home to interview a few folks and discover how other people saw succeeding and failing. He was to come back with more knowledge about the downside of success and the upside of failure.

The following week, Max raced into my office with great excitement. Waving papers in front of me, he exclaimed, "I got it—at least my mind does! I couldn't see it before—and I still can't wrap my head around it emotionally. Success really does have a downside, and failure does have some benefits. I'm still amazed."

Max proceeded to fill out the rest of his infinity loop:

Achievement

Strengths

achievement, praise, recognition, accolades, appreciation, wealth, happiness, enjoyment, satisfaction, self-esteem, pride, accomplishment, approval, love, respect, attention, kindness, colleagues, triumph, name recognition, fulfillment, contentment, gratitude, acknowledgment

Strengths

challenge, opportunity, learning, growth, re-examination, creativity, options, change of direction, new focus, exploration, adventure, more education, fresh beginnings, evolution, development, imagination, resourcefulness, innovation, originality, inspiration, motivation

Success   Failure

Weaknesses

exhaustion, irritability, short temper, harshness, insensitivity to others, prickliness, rudeness, arrogance, egotism, severity, manipulation, difficulty, impatience, being controlling, low energy, isolation, disconnection, loneliness, unhappiness, confusion

Weaknesses

being a loser, a dud, a has-been, unworthy, nameless, faceless, invisible, and lost; blame; embarrassment; poverty; anonymity; shame; humiliation; mortification; chagrin; fear; terror; anger; rage; self-pity; self-hatred; dread; anxiety; frustration; guilt; sadness

Max's insights were powerful. They broke through his polarity blindness and gave him enough flexibility to see his dilemma in a different way.

He didn't feel any great degree of difference—yet. But his mind was now open.

That completes Step One for Max.

Ragini's Map: Trust or Doubt?

Now let's look at an inner tug-of-war that I, and many others, have struggled with daily. The context where it plays out is faith; and in my case, the dilemma seemed to show up in almost every decision I had to make. I constantly asked: Should I follow my trusting heart and take a risk—spend my money, open and share my heart, and give my soul permission to lead the way and feel truly alive? Or should I follow my doubting mind and stay safe—hold on to my money, avoid debt, keep my defenses intact, and tuck my soul away where it can't get more tainted?

Whatever life decisions I had to make, each seemed to provoke a question of faith—in myself, in others, in God or the Larger Whole. It seemed I needed to believe in something larger than myself—and I didn't. It isn't that I believed in nothing. There was just a big blank where other folks had faith. I needed to take some risks.

I'd rejected a multitude of childhood beliefs already, but I still hadn't found anything I could really believe in. I had no clear criteria or guidance for how to make my life work. Perhaps that's why the idea that I was destined to be happy took such a long-term hold on me. I lacked the confidence and conviction to believe in anything else.

I concluded that the deeper issue was faith itself because most of my struggles were colored by this quandary. The quest for faith became the context for most of my life choices. Much like Max's dilemma, mine found its way into almost everything. I found my predicament deeply irritating. Like most of us, I just wanted to be happy, and this seemed to make everything so much more complicated! After doing the loop work I'm about to share, the struggle ceased to be a problem. Even though I still feel the inner tug-of-war in my body, it's no longer an upsetting issue.

The Root Polar Pair

In any case, I was, paradoxically, happy to begin understanding my own unhappiness. I began by searching for the root polarity at work. Many describe faith and doubt as the opposites in play. But if I had to find faith, my faith would have to include doubt—because that was mostly what I did—day and night, awake or asleep. As I explored, it looked like I didn't have much faith in anything—myself, others, God, the Mystery, or the notion of something larger than self. It seemed I didn't have a clue how to trust. So I realized trust and doubt made up the root polar pair, and faith was the context.

Having faith means you entrust something important to someone or something else for care. It means you rely on that someone or something to carry out your request. It means being confident they can and will. I didn't have much trust in myself, much less anyone or anything else.

Can She Fix It?

No matter what the situation—buying new jeans, presenting at a conference, or working out a problem with a friend—this inner tug-of-war between trust and doubt seemed to be part of it. I didn't know whether to trust my decisions or to doubt them—I had decision paralysis. It seemed clear the problem wasn't fixable—at least not by me.

I tried applying the mystic Sengsten's wisdom. Remember it? The mind's distress is created by making one part of a polarity better than its opposite. Sengsten said he had a better way, and that gave me hope—even though the hope lay in grasping a rather cryptic piece of guidance: "You can find your way out of your dilemma by relaxing into it."

Making one part of a polarity better than its opposite creates distress in the mind.

Is It Interdependent?

I practiced relaxing, and then I began inquiring about the nature of my problem. This led me to confirm that trust does indeed define itself by the absence of doubt. And doubt defines itself by the absence of trust. It seemed the dilemma really wasn't fixable. With trust and doubt interdependent, the problem was definitely an Unresolvable Dilemma. My infinity loop looked like this:

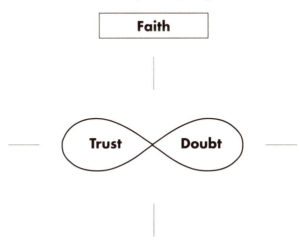

Trust and doubt are the two sides of the coin I call faith. To live with these two options driving both my faith and my lack of it, I had to learn more about what they were and how to manage them.

Being clear on that, I filled in the landmarks. They always let me know where I am as my dilemma plays out.

Strengths of Trust

Since I was more cynical and skeptical than trusting and accepting, I had to do a little research to find the strengths of trust. Most folks I knew called the strengths "gifts," which, at the time, made me scrunch my nose in distaste. I saw this label as presupposing some loving Giver of gifts. That was too New Age for me and became powerful food for my cynicism.

You can find your way out of your dilemma by relaxing into it.

Regardless, these were the strengths I assembled from talking to others. (Anytime you can't think of any strengths or weaknesses for one part of your polar pair, check out what others think—just like Max did.)

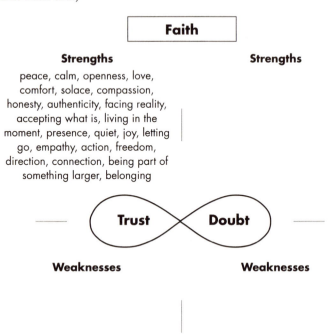

Faith

Strengths

peace, calm, openness, love, comfort, solace, compassion, honesty, authenticity, facing reality, accepting what is, living in the moment, presence, quiet, joy, letting go, empathy, action, freedom, direction, connection, being part of something larger, belonging

Strengths

Trust **Doubt**

Weaknesses **Weaknesses**

Weaknesses of Trust

Filling out the weaknesses of trust was much easier. I was prone to sneering at all of these landmarks, and when they snuck up on me and appeared in my own behavior, I ran straight into denial to get away from them, or I threw them at other people via blame:

Faith

Strengths

peace, calm, openness, love, comfort, solace, compassion, honesty, authenticity, facing reality, accepting what is, living in the moment, presence, quiet, joy, letting go, empathy, action, freedom, direction, connection, being part of something larger, belonging

Strengths

Trust ✕ **Doubt**

Weaknesses

being a Pollyanna, sugary sweet, saccharine, syrupy, passive, nonthinking, closed to new ideas, and controlling; blind faith; pushiness; anger; judgment; self-righteousness; superiority; pride; denial of reality; illogic; proselytization; insensitivity to others

Weaknesses

Strengths of Doubt

The strengths of doubt took some time for me to discover. I was so out of balance on this issue that I lived primarily in the weaknesses of both sides of the polarity. Trust was too dangerous, and doubt was too confusing. I unwittingly became a captive of cynical despair, which I trusted over anything else. I couldn't see that I had lost all touch with anything remotely positive.

Given the realities of our world, I viewed gratefulness as the height of absurdity. Little did I know that living at the height of absurdity makes daily life a much more workable proposition! I wasn't just a victim of polarity blindness like Max was. In spiritual terms, I was sound asleep to just about everything except my own private hell.

I had clearly polarized toward doubt and away from trust: but without knowing the strengths of doubt, I ended up spending most of my time on the downside of both loops. It was all a bit confusing—until I wrote out the strengths of doubt:

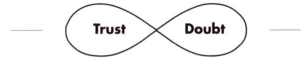

Faith

Strengths	**Strengths**
peace, calm, openness, love, comfort, solace, compassion, honesty, authenticity, facing reality, accepting what is, living in the moment, presence, quiet, joy, letting go, empathy, action, freedom, direction, connection, being part of something larger, belonging	inquiry, creativity, re-assessment, challenge, adventure, openness, new options, new direction, freedom, new strategy, openness, willingness, exploration, discovery, fun, excitement, imagination, inspiration, ingenuity, cleverness, motivation, stimulation, fun, involvement

Trust   **Doubt**

Weaknesses	**Weaknesses**
being a Pollyanna, sugary sweet, saccharine, syrupy, passive, nonthinking, closed to new ideas, and controlling; blind faith; pushiness; anger; judgment; self-righteousness; superiority; pride; denial of reality; illogic; proselytization; insensitivity to others	

I saw that doubt had value. This meant my dream of a faith that embraced doubt might be a real possibility. I was eager to continue on.

Weaknesses of Doubt

The weaknesses of doubt were much clearer to me, as they were practically my home address:

Faith

Strengths	**Strengths**
peace, calm, openness, love, comfort, solace, compassion, honesty, authenticity, facing reality, accepting what is, living in the moment, presence, quiet, joy, letting go, empathy, action, freedom, direction, connection, being part of something larger, belonging	inquiry, creativity, re-assessment, challenge, adventure, openness, new options, new direction, freedom, new strategy, openness, willingness, exploration, discovery, fun, excitement, imagination, inspiration, ingenuity, cleverness, motivation, stimulation, fun, involvement

Trust ⋈ **Doubt**

Weaknesses	**Weaknesses**
being a Pollyanna, sugary sweet, saccharine, syrupy, passive, nonthinking, closed to new ideas, and controlling; blind faith; pushiness; anger; judgment; self-righteousness; superiority; pride; denial of reality; illogic; proselytization; insensitivity to others	being critical, closed, attacking, argumentative, dismissive, sneering, and snide; skepticism; cynicism; judgment; arrogance; sarcasm; coldness; cruelty; unwillingness; defensiveness; rudeness; paralysis; anxiety; despair; hopelessness; fear; panic; helplessness; indecision

Discovering the strengths of both doubt and trust gave me hope. I hadn't known I was so lopsided in my perceptual ability. Being able to perceive some positivity opened the door to vast new possibilities.

If faith is also one of your primary dilemmas, repeat the steps, filling in the boxes with your own content. The beauty of the Six-Step Process is that you can use it with any content—as long as the issue is an Unresolvable Dilemma.

Your Map

Go back to the infinity loop you created earlier to map out the lay of the land in your Unresolvable Dilemma. You can use the checklist below to make sure you've covered all the aspects that make up the polarity in play.

- Situation
- Polar pair
- Is it unresolvable? Interdependent and inseparable?
- Strengths and weaknesses of one pole
- Strengths and weaknesses of the other pole

You have already identified the situation, or circumstance, in which the dilemma shows up. Now identify the polar pair at the root of your dilemma. Using our formula, make certain the opposites are interdependent. Write them inside the loops of the infinity symbol. If you need help, consult the Resources section. It contains lists of polar opposites in various contexts. One or more of them will pop out at you as the right set of opposites to work with.

Write down the strengths, or benefits, of one pole above its loop. Then underneath its loop, write down the weaknesses for that same experience—what comes when you stay focused on that pole *to the exclusion of its opposite.*

Write down the strengths, or benefits, of the opposite pole above its loop. Then underneath its loop, write down the weaknesses for that same experience—what comes when you stay focused on that pole *to the exclusion of its opposite.*

Congratulations! You have mapped out the lay of the land for your own Unresolvable Dilemma. You now have in front of you a map of what you want to move toward and what you want to move away from. You've also added landmarks (strengths and weaknesses) to help you find your way. Next, try a little experiment to see if your body agrees with your mind.

A Little Experiment

Place the infinity loop you drew and have filled in down on the floor. Stand on it right at the center point, so you have one loop to your right and the other to your left. Don't use the Three-Point Balancing Act you learned in chapter 7. Right now, just stand in the middle and focus on what you feel in your body.

Are you pulled toward one loop? Repelled by the other? Swaying back and forth between the two? Don't think! Just feel. If what you feel is the opposite of what you thought, just stay relaxed. Explore the lay of the land as it is right now. Learn what your body wants to move toward and what it wants to move away from. This tells you what your unconscious mind is doing.

When Maggie first did the Six-Step Process for the context of needs, she was certain she'd be pulled toward fulfilling other people's needs and away from fulfilling her own. When she stood on her loop, she was shocked. Her body practically fell over in the direction of her own needs. What's more, she felt a real repulsion for the loop that represented fulfilling other's needs.

Maggie's unconscious mind was now more interested in fulfilling her own needs than the needs of others. Feeling this in her body shed new light on why she had developed such a strong aversion to continuing the status quo. The pull to change things had gotten stronger than the pull to keep them the same. Maggie had habituated to pleasing others, but her unconscious mind was ready to rebalance the game.

This was good news for Maggie. She contemplated the possibility that there might be some force stronger than her conscious mind that was offering direction. Happily for her, it was pulling in the same direction she desired.

After you've checked out how *your* body responds to your dilemma, step off the infinity loop and bring your focus back to right here. Ready? Let's move on to Step Two.

12

STEP TWO—THE RIVER RUNNING THROUGH IT

TOOLS YOU'LL NEED FOR STEP TWO

*Your **willingness**: to perceive the unpleasant, scary parts of your dilemma as valuable and helpful*

Now you have a map of the lay of the land that is your Unresolvable Dilemma. It's shaped like the infinity loop; you've pinpointed all the landmarks (strengths and weaknesses) that identify it as your predicament. You know which parts are pleasant and which are unpleasant.

Step One was very personal. You brought out what's been going on in the privacy of your mind and put it on paper in front of you. This has created some distance so now you're free to perceive it from a different perspective.

Be aware that other people could have the same dilemma in the same context as what you're experiencing but could use different landmarks to identify it. Their experiences won't be the same as yours, and neither will their maps. So don't be confused if other people look at your map and disagree with your landmarks.

Step Two focuses on the defining feature of the Land of Unresolvable Dilemma—the river running through it. This feature isn't something you affect with your personal experience. It's completely impersonal. The river's characteristics don't change to accommodate you or your situation. The river is simply a part of the terrain.

You can't alter it, and you can't ignore it either.

HERE'S WHAT WE'RE GOING TO DO IN STEP TWO:

1. Draw arrows to indicate the unalterable direction of the river's flow

2. Highlight the hidden pattern of the river's flow between its two banks

3. Learn how to perceive the unpleasant, scary parts of the river as valuable and helpful

4. Uncover the paradox of competitive collaboration and understand how it keeps the river flowing

In the Land of Unresolvable Dilemma, the river is the only means of efficient and pleasant transportation. The river's banks, as well as the land, are covered with thorny thickets, blackberry brambles, swamps, quicksand, sinking bogs, quagmires, and hidden tar pits. Travelers who ignore the river often get lost and never return, so it's best to stay on the waterway and to learn as much as you can about it.

How the River Flows

The river is the flow of life itself—constantly moving and shifting. It is the flow of change. This flow moves in a certain direction and in a specific pattern. The best way to travel here is on the river, so it's wise to know its route and if there's anything dangerous to watch out for.

First, let's look at the route the river follows. Our mystics have mapped it out for us. They've made it quite predictable, and this knowledge helps create a safer and more secure journey.

The First Defining Feature of the River: The Direction of the Flow

Navigating this river is both easy and relaxing, and hard and challenging. But when you know where the river's going, you can follow its flow with a stronger degree of ease, comfort, confidence, and certainty.

Here's the direction: The river streams from the strengths of one pole *downward* into its own weaknesses. Then it moves from those weaknesses *up* into the strengths of the opposite pole. Then it flows *down* into the weaknesses of that pole—and then *up* into the strengths of the opposite pole. And so it goes again, and again, ad infinitum.

Achievement

Strengths

achievement, praise, recognition, accolades, appreciation, wealth, happiness, enjoyment, satisfaction, self-esteem, pride, accomplishment, approval, love, respect, attention, kindness, colleagues, triumph, name recognition, fulfillment, contentment, gratitude, acknowledgment

Strengths

challenge, opportunity, learning, growth, re-examination, creativity, options, change of direction, new focus, exploration, adventure, more education, fresh beginnings, evolution, development, imagination, resourcefulness, innovation, originality, inspiration, motivation

Weaknesses

exhaustion, irritability, short temper, harshness, insensitivity to others, prickliness, rudeness, arrogance, egotism, severity, manipulation, difficulty, impatience, being controlling, low energy, isolation, disconnection, loneliness, unhappiness, confusion

Weaknesses

being a loser, a dud, a has-been, unworthy, nameless, faceless, invisible, and lost; blame; embarrassment; poverty; anonymity; shame; humiliation; mortification; chagrin; fear; terror; anger; rage; self-pity; self-hatred; dread; anxiety; frustration; guilt; sadness

The Inevitability of Change

When I shared the direction of the river's flow with Maggie and Max, they each responded with the same question: "Why?" I gave them the same answer. "The reason is change. Remember the permanence of impermanence? Well, here are its effects in your daily life. Nothing can stay the same. Sooner or later, everything that arises also passes away."

Maggie vigorously nodded her head while simultaneously blurting out her protest, "Yes, but I don't want to have those weaknesses. They make me a bad person, and I hate them all!" Maggie's whole body engaged in an energetic foot stomp to express the intensity of her feelings. Her wild hairdo flopped around with her. For a moment she looked like one of those angry gnomes in fairy tales when they don't get their way and they stomp around enraged. She laughed at her own intensity but continued, "Why can't the river just flow back and forth between the strengths? That's change enough, isn't it?"

Max just looked at me, eyes wide open, staring straight ahead. After a moment or two, he said, "Are you saying the weaknesses I wrote up there are necessary? That they're going to be a part of my life regardless?"

These were excellent inquiries. When I first saw the direction of the river's flow, my cynicism exploded too. On a rant, I exclaimed, "This is the stupidest design possible! It's mean, cruel, and unkind. It's one more piece of evidence for why it's stupid to believe in a loving and just God."

Accepting the river's flow means coming face-to-face with the most basic fact of life—the fact of change. I asked Maggie and Max to find something that *wasn't* subject to change. Unhappily, they both reported failure.

Although few of us embrace this aspect of our reality with abounding joy, our experience verifies the inevitability of change. Whatever comes into existence does eventually, and automatically, move out of existing as it was—a breath, a day, a job, a family, a project, an object, a dream, a value, a belief, a life. Everything changes.

Releasing the Goal of Permanence

Maggie and Max weren't thrilled with the idea of embracing impermanence as a permanent fixture in their journey, but I pointed out the benefits of this action. Consciously relaxing into change as an ongoing daily practice frees you to keep moving with the river's flow, gracefully and efficiently. It also frees you to consciously interrupt your unconscious as it strives for the unreachable goal of having or feeling any one thing, without interruption, permanently.

There are obvious places where it's useful to focus on creating durability, stability, and lastingness—a product, a service, knowledge, and objects of art. But applying this focus to creating pleasant emotional and mental states in perpetuity creates a problem. Imagine that thrilling kiss lasting forever—you could never eat again!

When the goal is to make your positive, pleasant experiences and emotions last forever, you are sure to fail. That's the bad news. The good news is your negative, unpleasant experiences and emotions can't last forever either.

Maggie and Max were both delighted to hear the good news, though they still weren't pleased at the prospect of letting the good things slip out of their hands.

Step Two clarifies how this pattern of flow between opposites actually plays out; you can clearly see what it looks like, and feels like, in action.

Maggie summarized my words like this: "So you mean the strengths have to break down and take on the shape of something else? And it's probably going to be something I find unpleasant?"

I replied, "That's right. When the strengths start to wane because of impermanence, they take on the shape of experiences you've learned to call weaknesses. And generally, these don't feel nearly as good as what you just left behind. Not a happy thing! I know."

Maggie sighed and gave a sullen nod of the head. I quickly reminded her that all was not lost! Speaking gently, I prompted, "But remember, Maggie. There's a silver lining here. Thanks to the permanence of change, the weaknesses also have to change. And, thank goodness for us, they naturally change into the strengths of the opposite pole. That's a happy thing!"

She brightened up a bit, as did Max when we had a similar conversation.

Max remembered that the flow between opposites had a patterned rhythm. He offered this observation: "So I guess the strengths I listed on the opposite pole are also impermanent. So they would have to change too, wouldn't they? And according to you, the pattern would be to change into that same pole's own weaknesses—and so on and so on. Is that right?"

I was delighted Max saw the pattern so clearly. I replied, "You bet! And then the good news comes again. Those weaknesses naturally move into the strengths of the opposite pole—again—and so it goes round and round!"

Knowing the direction of the flow allows you to find the pattern hidden inside it.

Max looked happier than before and summed it up this way: "So, it's actually pretty good! You never have to stay any one place too long, and you get to go everywhere!"

> Everything is subject to change. Nothing gets to stay the same.

You Can't Avoid the Weaknesses

Initially, neither Maggie, Max, nor I were wild about having to experience the weaknesses of our polar pair. You probably prefer to avoid these unpleasant experiences too. In fact, you might even willingly forego the strengths of one pole entirely in order to avoid its weaknesses.

Maggie and Max

I asked Maggie and Max to cover up the top half of their loop for a minute, blocking the strengths from view. I asked if what remained in view—the weaknesses of both sides—were the experiences they worked hard to resist or avoid. They both wholeheartedly agreed. Next, I asked them to cover the bottom half of the loop, blocking the weaknesses. They each noticed how much happier they were to be with the strengths.

Again, Maggie's comment revealed her endearing honesty. "Now this is the right way to live." With a chuckle and a big grin she continued, "I'm serious! I want all these pleasant things and none of the unpleasant ones."

Max's comment was a bit different. Serious and contemplative, he reflected, "I see how willingness to experience it all would make for a calmer life and a bigger sense of success—no matter what happens."

By design, our human response to Unresolvable Dilemma is to try to eradicate the existence of the lower part of the loop. If we are successful, we believe the upper part of the loop will become permanent. We dedicate huge amounts of time and energy toward attempting to curtail the frustration and struggle arising from the lower part of the loop; we endeavor to influence, alter, or control situations, other people, ourselves, and even God.

Knowing the direction of the flow allows you to find the pattern hidden inside it.

Maggie wasn't at ease with her emerging understanding, even though she desperately wanted to stop feeling despair. Pensively, she observed, "I can envision how gracefully and efficiently I could manage change if I weren't always so depressed. The fact that there's a direction to the river's flow gives me some hope—but I'm still feeling lost." I could see there were a few remaining strings attaching Maggie to her old way of relating to opposites, which we would deal with soon.

On the other hand, Max was pulsing with excitement; he wanted to hurry up and keep learning more. He shared, "Now I can see there's a way out of my anxiety; I just need to understand exactly how success and failure work as a team. I'm really curious."

Ragini

When I realized I couldn't control the direction of the river's flow, I was truly annoyed. I did *not* want those weaknesses in my life! My need to be CEO of everything was seriously challenged. But as I relaxed and explored the value of the river's route, its unalterable directionality became a blessing—and a concrete element of predictability. In the midst of all the unending change, I eventually found this comforting and extremely useful.

Your Turn

Take a moment now to do this on your infinity loop. Cover up the top half of your loop. Focus on all the weaknesses, and notice how your body feels when you think about having to experience all these unpleasant landmarks. Do you resist and avoid them? Or relax and flow with them? Pass no judgments here. Just notice what is present in your body

Now cover the weaknesses and focus on the strengths. How do you feel about these? Do you want them to last forever? Are you willing to let them go when their time with you is over? Do you feel happy, angry, sad, confused? Don't judge it. Just be aware of what you feel and think and hang in there. There's more to learn.

Making Friends with Dilemma

The Six-Step Process is going to dissolve the struggle and frustration found in Unresolvable Dilemma. The emotional angst will disappear.

Understanding paradox doesn't make the dilemma go away, though. Instead, it changes how you feel about it and relate to it. With each step, you'll gain more peace around the issue and will have greater access to managing it successfully—your creativity and practical wisdom will guide the show.

Now let's take a look at another significant feature of our river.

The Second Defining Feature of the River: A Core Paradox Drives the Flow

Something unusual and fascinating evokes the current in this river. It's true that anytime water moves, there's a current. But the river's movement in the Land of Unresolvable Dilemma is patterned and, thus, repetitive. You can count on it to flow in the same direction you've just learned, over and over again. But what makes the current flow in this pattern?

The pattern is created by two life forces that shouldn't be complementary, but actually are. You probably won't be surprised that these two forces are a polar pair, composed of interdependent

> Opposites are fundamentally not in opposition. They are complementary.

and complementary opposites. Together, they create a core para-dox—the second defining feature of our river.

One force of this core paradox is the drive to change things and make them different. The opposing force is the drive to pre-serve things and make them stay the same.

It was important for Maggie and Max to personally verify this information. Did these two paradoxical forces function in their own lives? I asked Maggie if there were times when she wanted something to change but also to stay the same.

She responded quickly, "Oh my god, yes. I want immediate change right now. I want all these people who are in my life to get out of my life so no one can ask me for help. But at the same time, I don't want them to leave. I like having them around, and they bring me a lot of pleasure too—and self-esteem."

Max discovered there were a lot of things he wanted to stay the same but also change. "I want to stay successful, maintain my wealth, keep my gold card, and retain my reputation. This means eighty-hour work weeks, which I'm happy to do. At the same time, I want this to change. I want to take vacations with my family, to find new ways to express my passion, and spend a couple of days a week work-ing with my hands and being creative in a different way."

> *Two paradoxical life forces drive the flow of change: the drive to make things different and the drive to keep things the same.*

The Flow of Competitive Collaboration

When you struggle with an Unresolvable Dilemma, you can feel this inner tug-of-war in your body. What you're feeling is these two paradoxical life forces engaged in competitive collaboration. This is not an antagonistic battle, though. It is a harmonious part-nership.

This partnership drives the famous "on the one hand . . . but on the other hand" experience of dilemma, of the "should I do this

. . . or should I do that?" quandary. Your inner tug-of-war is your direct experience of the interaction between the drive to change and the drive to preserve. These two paradoxical life forces continuously interact, trying to influence your decision as to which option to choose—and simultaneously shaping you and your life.

The Mystical View of Opposites

I urged Maggie and Max to remember the words of our mystic guides. I reminded them that we were exploring the mystical view of opposites—the hidden wisdom that discontent reveals.

Maggie thought all the ideas were beautiful. But one afternoon, she shared quite wistfully, "I love these ideas and I really wish they could be true. But in my heart of hearts, I don't have much hope things can actually change for me. I think I'm just too damaged." Nevertheless, Maggie found her courage and wanted to keep on. Her wish was her only hope, and she dared to follow that slender thread a bit farther.

Max was still excited and wanted to know more. One morning he confided, "I love this stuff, but I'm scared I won't follow through. In my professional life, I never leave a goal unattended. But in my personal life, I'm usually quite willing to leave things undone and incomplete."

> Your inner tug-of-war is your direct experience of the interaction between the drive to change and the drive to preserve.

Max and Maggie were both describing interference to living their dreams. I assured them we'd deal with their fears and doubts when we got to Step Five. They were both relieved as I reminded them that everything they encountered on this journey was just a process of discovery, of what Unresolvable Dilemma actually is, how it works, why it's better to manage it than to try to get rid of it, and what's stopping them from going with the flow.

Now you've completed Step Two and are clear on the important aspects of the river: it moves in a certain direction with a specific pattern hidden inside its flow, and its current is driven by the movement between two paradoxical life forces.

Let's move on to why it's better to run the risk of the river's rapids than try to journey through the surrounding lands.

13

STEP THREE—RIDING THE RIVER'S RAPIDS

TOOLS YOU'LL NEED FOR STEP THREE

*Your **intention and willingness, curiosity, doubt** and **connection to a larger system:** so you can experience that bad times don't have to be avoided.*

Maggie's wish for all this mystical stuff to be true motivated her demand for a fuller explanation. What was the purpose of it?

In a challenging tone, she threw out the following questions: "I just don't get why this has to be the way it is. What's the reason for it? Okay, impermanence is a factor. But why can't we just get rid of the weaknesses? Isn't that what religion and spirituality are all about? Changing ourselves so the world can be a better place?"

Maggie grew up in a fundamentalist family. She rejected her parents' religion long ago, yet still hungered for a sense of larger purpose. On a deeply private level, she continuously searched for some sign of her significance in the world—why she was here, and what she was supposed to be doing.

HERE'S WHAT WE'RE GOING TO DO IN STEP THREE:

1. Envision the role of the Unresolvable Dilemma and its larger purpose

2. Explore personal meaning and significance and how paradoxical wisdom answers these concerns to quiet and calm your mind

3. Decode your discontent, finding wisdom for emotional calm

4. Appreciate managing opposites as the key to being unflappable in daily life

The Mystery of Living Systems

Although the Six-Step Process is rooted in mystic psychology, Step Three uses the language of science. Instead of talking about God, we talk about living systems theory,[8] an excellent blend of the verifiable and the mysterious.

I described living systems to Maggie and Max as simply as I could: "A living system, by definition, is an open structure that self-organizes as it moves and intermingles with the environment around it." I told Maggie she was a living system and I was a living system; and when we came together, the two of us automatically formed a larger living system. As living systems interact, they tend to grow more and more complex, creating larger and larger living systems. The following are some examples in different contexts:

- At home—the individual, couple, family, neighborhood, community

- At work—the individual, team, division, corporation, competition, industry

- Geographically—the house, neighborhood, city, county, state, country, continent, global community

- Environmentally—rain drop, puddle, pond, lake, stream, river, sea, ocean

- Human consciousness (noosphere[9])—individual, collective unconscious, collective conscious, integral, evolutionary, mystical

Somehow, life has the capacity to increase its complexity and still function.[10] That includes us.

Maggie wanted to know the purpose of these Unresolvable Dilemmas. If she could find a reason that made sense, she could more easily accept the river's flow—especially its path through the weaknesses. To answer her question, we had to look a little deeper.

How to Spot a Living System

Let's approach Unresolvable Dilemma as belonging to a Larger Living System, which acts as a sort of caretaker to all the smaller living systems within its scope. It is inseparable from them, creating a network of sorts. It looks like there's a head pooh-bah, but it's really a network where every part is equally important in creating the whole. Your body is a good example. All the components are equally important in creating a healthy, viable, whole living system called you.

This Larger Living System, like all the living systems it encompasses, has three primary directives:

1. Rebalance—homeostasis, or recreating balance.

2. Renewal—replenishing nourishment and energy.

3. Creative expansion—evolution and growth.

Imagine as if the fabric of our particular Larger Living System is composed of opposites. These opposites are interdependent and complementary, just as you've learned, and they compete with each other in a harmonious fashion via competitive collaboration. These are all the elements that make up our Unresolvable Dilemmas.

The Role of Your Unresolvable Dilemmas

Does the Unresolvable Dilemma play a particular role in our Larger Living System? Yes, it does. Imagine as if Unresolvable Dilemma is the primary operating strategy (the how-to-get-there steps) for reaching the fundamental goals of all living systems—rebalance, renewal, and creative expansion.

What does it use to reach these objectives? The conflict and friction you experience in the presence of Unresolvable Dilemma—that frustrating and uncomfortable inner tug-of-war.

Remember, that felt sense of conflict is the result of the two basic paradoxical life forces—the drive to preserve and the drive to change—interacting in their game of competitive collaboration. This friction is actually creativity in disguise, which is essential to accomplishing the goals.

Riding the River's Rapids: Your Emotional Ups and Downs

That's pretty clever, isn't it? Viewed from this perspective, everything you've learned about opposites has a purpose and a function that makes our lives what they are. Furthermore, *you*, as a living system, play a pivotal role in helping the Larger Living System reach its three basic goals—rebalance, renewal, and creative expansion. And you are especially helpful when you travel with the river's flow.

Going against that flow, or trying to travel on the surrounding lands, turns that harmonious tension and conflict into discord. (Of course, in the Land of Unresolvable Dilemma, discord paradoxically plays a role in creating the harmony—it's not a bad thing. It's just not as much fun for you.) When you leave the loop, you forget your map and your wisdom. You move as if you are not a part of the whole. In this scenario, the system can no longer balance, renew, and create as easily as when you stay with the river's flow.

This situation creates confusion for the errant traveler's energies. Without the direction and force of the river's flow to guide her, the energies become antagonistic. Now tinged with fear, she starts to serve greed, hatred, and destruction. The ups and downs of the Unresolvable Dilemma, its swirling rapids and steep falls, become unmanageable and begin generating blocks and barricades and twisting infinity loops whenever opposites come into play.

It is your choice whether to travel by land, avoiding the river, or to stay on the river and go with its flow. But be aware! Anytime you try to avoid, change, or manipulate the river's flow, your discomfort and pain will, sooner or later, spiral into suffering—usually defined as the emotional pain created by rejecting the pain already there, instead of relaxing into it. Riding the river's rapids—the emotional ups and downs of the strengths and weaknesses—makes the journey much easier. And it's quite doable when you understand their role in creating equilibrium, stability, fresh energy, and new expressions of life.

Maggie and Max thought all this made good sense. I was ready to move on to Step Four when Maggie asked a profound question—a question whose answer inevitably requires faith in something: "Why is this Larger Living System made up of opposites? Why not make it something else that's not so complex or confusing?"

A Mystical Assumption

To answer her question, we had to take a moment to step into the fundamental assumption of most religions and all spirituality: there is only one God, or one Universe, or one Whole that encompasses *everything* that exists.

Whether you accept or reject this premise, a felt sense of Oneness is the aim of the mystical path. It's not, as Maggie implied earlier, about getting rid of all your weaknesses so the world can be a better place—even though that's a strong belief most of us still think is the goal. It's about seeing that the world—and you—is already a magnificent mystery, *and* working to make it even better—even though, paradoxically, it's perfect as it is.

Maggie was quite aligned with this Oneness idea and kept looking more alert and engaged. Max seemed to withdraw a little, indicating he rarely thought about such things. I assured him he didn't need to believe in God or to chase after Oneness to reap the benefits of the Six Steps. He relaxed, gave a big sigh of relief, and chuckled as he said, "Thank God!"

Opposites: Our Bridge to Oneness

So why does our world have to be made of opposites—or what's also called duality—and not something else? Many traditions and cultures have stories to answer the question, but the actual answer isn't knowable by the mind. However, giving the mind the know-how to live with opposites and paradox gives you peace of mind, a truly loving heart, and a willing spirit, free to finally soar.

> Opposites are fundamentally not in opposition. They are Oneness in disguise.

If you long for a felt sense of spiritual connection (Oneness), you may be similar to Maggie. The experience of Oneness had been blocked from her awareness. Fundamentally, this was the result of not knowing how to successfully navigate the twoness she kept meeting along the way.

This twoness is the flow between opposites. It creates the paradoxical nature of our human experience. It creates the Unresolvable Dilemmas that force you to choose between only two options over and over again. This takes us back to the beginning. If there's a *me*, there has to be a *you*. You can't have *self* without *other* to give it meaning. Likewise, you can't have *one* without *two* to provide its definition.

Your mind's eye is not trained to see this. How many times in a week do you figuratively and unconsciously point your finger and in some way imply, "They're responsible for this," effectively dividing your world into an us-versus-them situation?

Your mystic's eye naturally perceives the hidden harmony between opposites. In so doing, the mysterious Oneness comes out of hiding and stands in plain view—even though the polar pair is still there. *This perception is the missing link in practical spirituality.*

It connects your human self and your divine self in the everyday affairs of life.

Most spiritual paths call our world the realm of duality (opposites, or twoness), and the spiritual world the realm of Oneness. Mystics say both realms exist simultaneously. You can begin to manage this paradox when you no longer try to find Oneness by trying to get rid of twoness—or setting up what you like against what you dislike, creating the perception of a problem.

Your mystic's eye naturally perceives the hidden harmony between opposites.

Opposites: Illusion or Reality?

With a slightly rebellious intensity, Maggie voiced a thoughtful and weighty question—one that remains a source of confusion for many spiritual seekers: "What about this spiritual teaching that says the duality in our world is an illusion, that all the distinctions we make between good and bad, pleasant and unpleasant, right and wrong are false because there only exists this one Whole?"

I replied, "Actually, Maggie, that is true—*if* you are looking at life from outside your mind and outside the realm of conceptual thought."

Maggie paled and looked a little panicked. I quickly continued, "But it's a paradox, Maggie. Duality, opposites, and distinctions are *both* an illusion *and* very real. Our universe operates on a polarity principle. You can't get away from polar pairs and their love affair. To verbalize truth from the mystical view, it has to be paradoxical."

Maggie looked totally confused. Her hand gestured me to stop, and she asked yet another probing question. "You mean, we live in two worlds? One is thinking about life, and the other is directly experiencing it—without your mind judging its beauty or ugliness or rightness or wrongness?"

Happily, I replied, "Maggie, you're brilliant! That's exactly it. When you look at opposites using your mind's eye, they look opposed, antagonistic, and in a real fight. But using your mystic's eye, they appear complementary and in a harmonious dance. This view allows you to relax and more easily step aside from your mind's story about whatever has just happened. But . . . you still have to manage the world of opposites."

Good versus Evil

When you're trying to figure out what you believe in and how to deal with all the conundrums of our world, the question of good and evil inevitably arises. People deal with this in many ways, ranging from denial that it's an issue to the extreme polarization of working to eradicate one so the opposite is all that's left.

Maggie

Having been raised in a fundamentalist family, Maggie still had great concerns about evil. She said, "But surely you're not saying evil doesn't exist, are you? It's obvious that evil is real."

It's a question most everyone asks, and it requires an answer. I can tell you what I told Maggie, but you have to work this question out for yourself in your own way.

Here's my reply to Maggie: "Of course evil exists, as does good—and to the mind's eye it looks like they're in a fight to the death. The mystic's eye sees them existing as well, but it perceives them in a different way. If you use the infinity loop, the mystical perspective places good as a strength and evil as a weakness of *another* polar pair—the light and dark sides of being human."

Maggie jerked up in her chair and took a deep breath. I continued, "When a person does something evil, he is seen as seriously stuck on the downside of the loop. That means he has no awareness of opposites as complementary and interdependent or working in a harmonious partnership. It means he's following a disastrous route—trying to fix an Unresolvable Dilemma rather than managing it."

From the mystical view, evil arises when a person is completely unaware of opposites as one unified Whole. If you look to the wisdom of your discontent, it points out that evil rests in first setting up what you like against what you dislike, and then dedicating all action to the permanent eradication of what stops you from getting what you want—calling that good.

Understanding this took Maggie a few moments, but she came a few steps closer to accepting the reality of opposites and the pattern of movement between them. She was suddenly smiling. I think her mind was busily, and happily, wrapping itself around this alternate way of seeing evil—a way that left her more able to breathe and relax.

I was quiet for a minute or two and then added, "Here's the paradox, Maggie: You can accept good and evil as two polar opposites playing their role in the harmonious and competitive collaboration of the light and the dark sides of being human. Remember the weaknesses on the downside of the loop? They're actually transitional stages that you'll learn more about in Step Five. These experiences play an important role in rebalancing, renewing, and expanding the living system. This way of seeing good and evil can help you relax, find a place of inner peace, and simultaneously honor their battle on this plane and take whatever action you feel you need to take."

Maggie summed up the possible impact of this kind of understanding. She said, "It seems when I use this mystical view, I can stop thinking my role is to rid the world of evil, and I can put more of my focus on being a beacon of light in this darkness. Is that the point? Shifting the way I see it shifts the way I feel?"

I couldn't have said it better. Maggie now had an alternative way to handle this age-old question. With it came some peace, clarity, and more motivation to live her life the way she wanted to—with love, compassion, and joy taking the lead.

Max

Max had only a passing interest in this question of spiritual versus human, and good versus evil. And that wasn't a problem. As I said earlier, you don't have to be deeply interested in purpose and meaning to use the Six-Step Process and get results.

Ragini

When I faced the question of what to do with evil, a famous poem by the mystic Rumi helped me a lot:

> *Out beyond ideas of wrongdoing and rightdoing there is a field. I'll meet you there.*

That place of "wrongdoing and rightdoing" is the territory of the mind or conceptual reality, the place where Unresolvable Dilemma is located, where good and evil make their home. The field beyond is where life itself happens—before your mind describes it, making it personal, and creating a story about its rightness or wrongness. Nature is full of creation and destruction, but most of us don't call tornadoes, hurricanes, and earthquakes right or wrong, or good or evil. They're simply acts of nature, of life.

Rumi continues with what happens when you enter this magical place just beyond the mind:

> *When the soul lies down in that grass, the world is too full to talk about.*

He then affirms the reality of paradoxical experience:

> *Ideas, language, even the phrase* each other *doesn't make any sense.*

You

How about you? How do you feel about the question of good versus evil? About having two sets of eyes that see different things simultaneously? Just notice what you're feeling now and what emotions or thoughts come up as you read on. And remember, you're just exploring. Nothing you find is good or bad. It's just what's there.

Two Seemingly Opposed Realities
Side-by-Side

There you are, lying in the field with Rumi "out beyond ideas of wrongdoing and rightdoing" and the twoness of the situation (you and Rumi) is undeniable. Yet, this distinction makes no sense when you're seeing with your mystic's eye. The Oneness is obvious. Hence, the paradox: you can perceive both dimensions at the same time—human and divine.

Living in the world of opposites requires making distinctions, for sure. But that doesn't happen in this field that lies beyond the concepts of the mind. There is no need in that quiet space between thoughts. It all comes down to a small shift in perception. Are you using your mind's eye? Or are you using your mystic's eye? When *both* perceptions become available, you are free to live with *both* of your dimensions as co-creators.

Both perspectives are real and yours to enjoy. The mind's perspective gives you a way to dream and to actualize your dream. The mystic's perspective gives you a bridge to the territory of life beyond thoughts, ideas, and concepts—beyond achievement and doing. It gives you the feel of a different kind of ground to stand on, located just to the side of your mind.

Without your mystic's eye, it's hard to find a way out of your mind's thoughts and their copious by-products—emotional chaos, emotional turmoil, and emotional pain and suffering. But with your mystic's eye, you can perceive the concepts of *false* and *true* traveling together, as well as *illusory* and *real* journeying side by side. You know they are inseparable and one organic unified whole. That's when inner peace and that different brand of happiness arrive.

When Maggie heard these words, she began to cry—quietly and softly, tears of both joy and sorrow. This is a common reaction when we meet these notions head on. How can everything we experience be both an illusion and reality—simultaneously?

Of course, the answer is paradox.

Be Kind to Your Body-Mind

Whether opposites and this plane of reality are illusory or real, you can bet your last dollar your body and mind find them very real. Body and mind are subject to the fabric of their environment, and that fabric is composed of a world of opposites.

Whether our world is real or illusory, it is a great kindness to your body and mind to understand the nature of paradox. Embracing this wisdom is truly an act of self-love—a compassionate gesture of kindheartedness toward your self—that mysterious force breathing you alive and giving you the gift of yet another moment, another hour, another day as a paradoxical being, simultaneously both human and divine, free to play with your potential to generate light or darkness.

Paradox is the thread knitting the fabric of all your spiritual and psychological insights together. Learning this Six-Step Process gives you the knowledge to navigate paradox via the wisdom of your discontent—and that includes how to live *with* paradox—and how to live *in* paradox.

Maggie remained hesitant about believing in any kind of God or Wholeness. She wanted to, desperately, but her fear of again feeling duped and disappointed ran strong. She didn't trust her desire to relax into something larger than herself.

On the other hand, once Max got past feeling uncomfortable with the topic, he surprised himself. He discovered he *did* actually believe in something larger than himself. He didn't have a name for it, but he experienced it often when he was on stage, presenting, and also when he was out on his boat.

At this point, both Maggie and Max had enough of their deeper philosophical questions answered to continue. They were ready to find out what was specifically interfering with their ability to go with the river's flow. If you're ready too, let's move on to Step Four.

14

STEP FOUR — OBSTACLES TO YOUR ENJOYABLE TRAVEL

TOOLS YOU'LL NEED FOR STEP FOUR

*Your **curiosity, intention,** and **willingness:** to understand the energy of the resistance in the body-mind.*

To become unflappable and gracefully navigate Unresolvable Dilemma on a daily basis, you have to use the wisdom of your discontent. This entails being ready, able, and willing to travel everywhere on your infinity loop. Maggie and Max soon discovered they weren't as open to this process as they had thought—nor as willing as they had hoped. How about you? Are you ready to let yourself go with the flow and move completely around your loop? Let's check it out.

HERE'S WHAT WE'RE GOING TO DO IN STEP FOUR

1. Identify obstacles to going with the flow of the river
2. Distinguish obstacles from the heightened emotional charge attached to them
3. Discover biology's hardwired drive to avoid emotional pain
4. Explore moving from emotional reaction to reflection

Finding Your Obstacles

The obstacles are those landmarks you wrote down in Step One that you really do *not* want to experience.

Maggie

I asked Maggie to revisit all the landmarks she identified on her loop—both the strengths and the weaknesses of both sides. I requested she notice where she felt any unwillingness in her body, no matter what kind: repulsion, numbness, paralysis, anxiety, fear, terror—or resistance of any kind, to any degree. I had her put a star by anything she didn't want to feel, really didn't want to deal with, or desperately wanted to say no to! Here's what she starred:

Weaknesses of Fulfilling Others' Needs: *hopelessness, doom, indifference, laziness, meaninglessness, purposelessness, feeling lost, abandonment, bitterness, hatefulness, harshness, hostility, vicious thoughts, envy*

Weaknesses of Fulfilling Her Own Needs: *guilt, selfishness, greed, huge ego, self-importance, self-indulgence, arrogance, cockiness, egotism, haughtiness, being too big for your britches, pride, overconfidence, being a bad person, ugliness, cruelty, unkindness, unfriendliness, solitude, resentment, pressure*

As you can see, Maggie had a lot of resistance to experiencing many of the weaknesses.

Max

When I asked Max to revisit the landmarks he'd identified, he got very antsy. He had drawn his loop on a piece of butcher paper pinned to a wall. As he stood in front of it, he started to shift from one foot to the other; a bead of sweat even popped up on his brow.

Success having a downside and failure having an upside were new concepts to Max. Just looking at the words he'd written made him very nervous. He didn't find anything to star in the weaknesses of success. Although these were mostly unpleasant states, he saw them as part of the success story—unpleasant but needed to keep him on track. His body wasn't resistant to any of them.

But the weaknesses of failure were another matter. Here's what he starred:

Weaknesses of Failure: *being a loser, a dud, a has-been, unworthy, nameless, faceless, invisible, and lost; anonymity; shame; humiliation, mortification; chagrin; fear; terror; self-pity; self-hatred; sadness; unhappiness; worthlessness*

Max began to understand why he felt so much panic and terror around failure. He didn't have a clue how to handle any of the things he feared.

Ragini

Most of my obstacles were landmarks on the strengths part of my loop. At first I was confused. How could I be resisting pleasant things that would hopefully make me happy? I realized I was scared of these things too. Believing myself to be a cynical soul, this much positivity felt like garlic must smell to the vampire. I just had to run.

As I focused on the words I'd written, my body recoiled. Many people are in terror of their own goodness, love, and compassion. The light side of being human can be as hard to swallow as the dark side.

Here's what I starred:

Strengths of Doubt: *creativity, challenge, adventure, openness, new options, new direction, freedom, willingness, exploration, discovery, fun, excitement, inspiration, ingenuity, involvement*

Strengths of Trust: *openness, love, solace, accept what is, quiet, joy, letting go, empathy, freedom, connection, a part of something larger, belonging, optimism, positivity, conviction, surrender, receptivity*

The weaknesses of doubt, unpleasant as they were, equaled my identity. I truly believed they accurately described the real me; nothing got a star there.

On the other hand, the landmarks on the downside of trust made me run like the devil. The idea of being sweet made me nauseous. It sounds extreme, but it was the truth. My aversion to

the notion of unconditional love, sentimentality, and what I perceived as sappy emotions was funny, considering my lifelong bent
for tragic romance.

> **Weaknesses of Trust:** *being a Pollyanna, sugary sweet,*
> *saccharine, syrupy, passive, nonthinking, and closed to new*
> *ideas; blind faith; denial of reality; illogic; proselytization;*
> *insensitivity to others*

You

Now it's your turn. Go to your infinity loop and make a star by
every landmark you wrote down that you don't want to experience.
My recommendation: be ruthlessly honest with yourself. In the
long run, it pays off. No one else needs to know what you're doing
here, but if you want to go with the flow, you need to know what's
stopping you. If you don't want to do this step, ask yourself what's
preventing you. Any obstacle you can identify will be helpful.

The Real Obstacle: Your Heightened Emotional Charge

Now that you've identified what's interfering with your willingness to move all the way around the infinity loop, I have a big
surprise for you. The obstacles you identified are *not* the actual
problem. The real problem is the heightened emotional charge you
feel *about* the obstacle.

You naturally want to avoid painful emotions. The ones that
feel good, you naturally want to keep. When strong emotions aren't
processed or expressed in some way, they keep expanding and getting stronger and stronger—like a popcorn kernel sizzling in oil,
quivering in anticipation of exploding. Just thinking of the experience you connect with the emotion can throw you into a panic, or
a paralysis, or an amazingly ecstatic daydream—like when you fall
in love or find a spiritual teacher or master. It's the same process
whether you're feeling ecstasy or agony.

Life's Emotional Ups and Downs

Without a map to navigate your emotional life, it can be quite an unpleasant ride. Remember that amusement park puzzle from Part One? It had a piece with a picture of a roller coaster on it? We talked about throwing it away because the ride made you sick to your stomach. Unlike that puzzle piece, you can't avoid the emotional roller coaster that equals being human.

No matter how hard you try, you can't get off the ride. Chaos and turmoil tinged with fear are simply emotional reality—but dealing with them is much easier when you have a way to peacefully ride the ups and the downs.

Max thought his boating experiences might be similar to a peaceful ride on that roller coaster. "It must be like riding the crest and trough of each wave when I'm out on my boat. I can't control the waves. They come, and they go. Some are little and weak, while others are big and strong—and scary. Once I understood this rhythm, I could relax and just go

Life will always give you emotional ups and downs.

with the boat's movement—up and down, up and down. It made my time out on the water a lot more fun and peaceful."

Max had it right. Just like waves, our emotions rise and fall without our say—as do the sun, the Dow, and the temperature. Maggie immediately agreed with wholehearted enthusiasm: "I feel so vindicated. I've been telling my family and friends that for years! But they keep saying I'm wrong and I should be able to control my emotions."

I wanted to be clear with Maggie on this point. "Emotions do just arise, Maggie. You're right. You can't control that. But after they've arrived, there is a way to manage them so they aren't the sole factor determining how you behave or how you make decisions. A life run solely by emotions is as out of balance as a life run solely by logic."

Because Maggie described her outer life as a hideous mess and her inner life as a muddle of fear and confusion, she wanted to learn how to do this seemingly impossible task—manage her emotions.

Max expressed delight at hearing that emotional folks could be out of balance too. He said, "That makes me feel a lot better. I thought emotional people always knew what they were doing with their emotions. Now I don't feel so stupid."

Emotions drove both Maggie and Max. Maggie knew it. She felt them pulling and pushing her all over the place. Max hadn't realized it. He was too busy running after success and avoiding failure to spend any time noticing his feelings. Neither had a clue what to *do* with their emotions or what they were really about.

Hardwired Reactions

Emotions are the grand challenge. They make us feel—but they make us feel both good and bad. They bring us both up (happy and alive) and down (unhappy and downhearted). Remember? It is a natural, hardwired, biological reaction to move away from pain of any kind *and* to cling to pleasure of any kind, including emotions.[11]

Generally, you may try to keep the *up* feeling by reveling in it. You attempt to prolong its presence. You hold on to the conversation with the friend, the lovemaking, the kiss, the romantic glance, the mountaintop view, the sunset, the creative flow, the career, the six-figure bank account, the recognition and kudos, the bliss of a moment. As you've now learned, this strategy generates suffering and disappointment because everything that arrives in your life will also eventually depart.

The usual way to handle the down feeling is to get away from it as quickly as possible and to avoid further contact. I used eating, watching TV or movies, reading a book, meditating, chatting with good friends in hundreds of different coffee shops all around the world, and, of course, overworking as ways to avoid the down feeling. Max played computer games, listened to music, had a few drinks, exercised, went out on his boat, and, yes, overworked. Maggie cooked oh so many good things, made love, traveled, entertained, and—that's right—overworked.

None of these activities are inherently bad. Yet, they can take on an unpleasant hue of dread when used as an escape from unpleasant emotions. Whatever you're trying to avoid is just around the corner, still waiting to get your attention. But now—you know there's no way to get rid of it for good.

Wisdom dictates that happiness and peace of mind easily arise when you embrace both emotional pleasure and emotional pain—and the continual flow of change surrounding them both. To do this requires some reflection. The big question is, *How do you move from reacting to your emotions toward reflecting on their presence?*

From Emotional Reaction to Reflection

To their own surprise, both Maggie and Max had an answer. They each went back to basics.

Maggie started at the beginning. "If I go back to where we started, I know that up and down emotions create a polar pair, and I think they're actually an interdependent pair. *Up* defines itself by the absence of *down*. *Down* defines itself by the absence of *up*. So this means they're inseparable. Whenever up arises, down will soon follow. And whenever down arises, up will soon follow. If I take the time to see it this way, I'll be reflecting rather than reacting, right?" Maggie had used her mystic's eye, and she was completely right on.

Max came up with this: "If I remember correctly, my negative emotions are just part of the flow between the two polar opposites, so I can relax and not run away. I know they're not going to last forever. Then I'll have more time to reflect on what they're trying to tell me, rather than reacting and running away. Then the two polar opposites can cooperate without me in the way and get the job done more effectively. Right?"

I loved Max's rendition, including his continued focus on achievement. I congratulated both of them on how well they were using some of the tools they'd brought on this journey: their curiosity, conscious awareness, intention, imagination, and doubt.

But to use what Max and Maggie remembered, you have to have more awareness than negative emotion. For most of us, that's simply not the case—especially when you're busy resisting what is actually happening.

You can build your awareness by relaxing into your resistance. In Step Six, you'll get more guidance for how to increase your attentiveness and alertness. But right now, the most important question is, How do you decrease the heightened emotional charge so you can move from reaction to reflection and become unflappable?

> To move from reacting to your emotions to reflecting on their presence decreases the heightened emotional charge.

How to move from reacting to reflecting is the penultimate piece of your discontent's wisdom. Step Five will guide you in doing this. You'll need the rest of those tools you packed in your bag back in chapter 9: willingness, conviction, and connection. Pull them out of your suitcase, and let's continue on.

15
STEP FIVE—THE NEW PERSPECTIVES FOR YOUR JOURNEY

TOOLS YOU'LL NEED FOR STEP FIVE

*Your **willingness, conviction, doubt,** and **connection to a larger system:** to experience and dissipate the resistance*

Now you know it's your emotional turmoil that is the real obstacle to going with the flow of life. This heightened emotional charge, which is attached to what you thought was the obstacle, is the real object of concern.

HERE'S WHAT WE'RE GOING TO DO IN STEP FIVE

1. Learn three tips for a quick release of your emotional turmoil
2. Apply tips to release emotional turmoil and move from reaction to reflection
3. Expand your notion of who you are
4. Embrace the value of your emotional turmoil
5. Test that your emotional turmoil has been released
6. Discover the mystical strategy for inner peace

Going back and forth between your dilemma's two options, weighing the pros and cons, creates emotional confusion. You're unable to choose either option with confidence and comfort. If you're already convinced one of the options is the only right choice (there's that tricky polarization again), you'll be busy grasping for the good one and avoiding the bad one.

Step Five teaches you three precise and proven tips for how to use your mystic eye's perspective to reduce this heightened emotional charge—easily and quickly. These tips give you three alternate ways to view the landmarks you've starred as obstacles. First, let's look at what these new viewpoints are. Then we'll learn how to use them.

Weaknesses Are Just Waning Strengths

You're probably already familiar with this viewpoint. The landmarks you wrote down on the bottom part of the infinity loop are actually the strengths of one pole *in the process of changing* into the strengths of the opposite pole. Because there's nothing you can do to alter this flow between opposites, it's in your best interest to understand it as fully as you can.

The two paradoxical life forces (the drive to change and the drive to keep things the same) push and pull the energies forward. Simultaneously, the energies flow back and forth between opposites: joy and sorrow, freedom and responsibility, separation and connection, acceptance and rejection, approval and criticism, and so on. This movement between polar opposites necessitates a phase when your life energy is neither one pole, nor the other. The energy is not well-formed; it is in a *transitional stage* as it changes from one form into its opposite. The wisdom of your discontent calls this transitional stage between opposites the waning of the strengths. You've been taught to call them weaknesses.

The wisdom of your discontent calls this transitional stage between opposites the waning of the strengths. You've been taught to call them weaknesses.

These waning strengths are generally unpleasant experiences, or at least uncomfortable ones. We think of them as making us weak. And of course, we've been taught that is bad, or at the very least, highly undesirable.

Back to Opposites 101! Remember Sengsten's wisdom: setting up what you like against what you dislike creates dis-ease. You've already discovered this to be true when you're dealing with an Unresolvable Dilemma. Unless your unconscious mind is offered a different option, it will automatically search for strength and try to avoid anything perceived as weakness.

In reality, these waning strengths are crucial—as are all transitional states—for the following reasons:

- Transitional states create a bridge between what was and what is coming.

- They never last.

- Their bridging provides an essential service to the two paradoxical life forces driving the movement.

- Transitional states keep your life energy freshly flowing from one pole to its opposite, rebalancing and renewing in the process.

Weaknesses Are Signals

The second tip helps you greet the weaknesses with gratitude! It says use your mystic eye and you'll perceive the weaknesses as actual signals sent to you from either the headquarters of your personal living system or from the Larger Living System.

When you perceive the weaknesses as signals, you can relax and acknowledge their message. What is that message? Simply put: "It's time to let go of where you've been and move on to the opposite pole! Rebalance! Renew! Expand!"

Max reacted to this like a kid who'd just been given a free ticket to the circus. He couldn't contain his excitement. Beaming, he leaped up out of his chair and almost began hopping around the room.

"You've got to be kidding! This is great! I can't believe it! You mean there's really something concrete and certain about these emotions? There's really some reason they're there? There are rules to the emotion game? Wow! If I learn the rules of the game, I can join in on the playing field and not get run over. This is big!" He grinned from ear to ear. His fear of failing in the emotional world had just taken an enormous hit.

Maggie, on the other hand, was very skeptical. Snorting with a tinge of cynical amusement, she laughingly said, "Signals? All this pain and suffering to just give me a signal?" She threw her hands up in the air and sneered, "Doesn't sound very efficient to me. Couldn't this larger system send the message in a less stressful way? I know burning bushes wouldn't work anymore, but how about a celestial email, or a fax from on high?" Suddenly she couldn't stop laughing; it was one of those hilarity fits when you laugh so hard you cry.

After a minute or so, she regained some control and said, "I feel like Dorothy in the Land of Oz. If weaknesses are a potent force with a powerful message, I'm definitely in the land of the weird. But, strangely enough, I do feel better now."

Weaknesses are, by design, immediate guidance for finding your location on the loop, *and* they tell you what to do so you don't get stuck there and end up fighting against the flow. Behaviorally, the message translates into these directions: Breathe. Relax. Let go.

Transitional states keep your life energy freshly flowing from one pole to its opposite, rebalancing and renewing in the process.

This is nature's way of keeping things fresh, renewed, and improved. This also applies to the strengths on your loop. They're signals as well—with one additional message: Breathe. Relax. Let go. And enjoy.

When you ignore the signals, unwittingly or consciously, you block the flow. This invites the infamous power struggle to enter the scene—between two parts of you, or between you and another: lover, partner, friend, child, parent, boss, organization, or even God.

Unawareness of your unconscious mind's resistance to the weaknesses acts as a blockage and causes various things to happen: You can get stuck in the downside of the pole you prefer. Then, like both Maggie and Max, you find yourself unsuccessfully scrambling to get back up to its strengths—like the Greek myth of Sisyphus, condemned to pushing a boulder up a mountain, only to watch it tumble back down to the bottom, again and again. Or, more like me, you can start getting all the weaknesses of *both* poles without getting *any* of the benefits of either—becoming a bit like Eeyore in *Winnie the Pooh*, always seeing the downside of everything.

> Weaknesses are (1) the waning of the strengths and (2) signals to rebalance, renew, and expand.

Both scenarios tend to place blame on someone or something outside of yourself. Thus, a power struggle ensues, complete with anger, resentment, and the goal of fixing the problem by fixing someone else. (I know this inside and out—and it's not pretty!)

The act of recognizing weaknesses as signals that the system is moving into imbalance frees your ability to manage this Unresolvable Dilemma. The downside? No one is happy that unpleasant experiences are a certainty in life. But this is one of those places where there are no bargains, no compromises, and no deals. The upside? Once you understand what's happening, you can leave power struggles behind. Power struggles only arise when you try to deal with an Unresolvable Dilemma by fixing it rather than managing it.

Knowing how to perceive these unpleasant experiences as signals changes everything. Being willing to enter and move through all of your identified weaknesses means a more efficient use of your own energy—mentally, emotionally, physically, and spiritually.

Perceiving weaknesses as the waning of strengths and as signals are two of the magical perceptions that reduce and release the heightened emotional charge clinging to those unwanted experiences. The next is the most powerful one yet.

Weaknesses Are Not Your Identity

This third shift in perception opens the door to a great sense of freedom. This tip has produced immediate release for thousands of people from a burden they didn't know they carried. Achieve this new perception by asking these three questions:

1. What if the weaknesses on the bottom part of the loop were not statements about who you are?

2. What if all of those weaknesses were just experiences to discover and explore?

3. What if none of them, in any way, were a comment on your identity, value, worth, or goodness?

All of a sudden Maggie looked jubilant, shocked, and shy—all at the same time. She whispered timidly, "Do you think that could really be true?" Just hearing the possibility made her stagger. A series of contorted looks passed swiftly over her face revealing all kinds of thoughts and feelings as they rearranged themselves inside.

Max was also astounded. He shared, "I've heard about this concept, but I didn't really understand how it could impact my life. I've always believed success in career and finances and social standing was a measure of who you are—your identity. If what you're saying is true, it's a wonderful relief—and kind of scary."

Both weaknesses and strengths are mistakenly used as indicators of our total identity rather than our personality's experience. Because of this confusion, we tend to say, "Yes, I was successful at that. Therefore, *I am* a success. Oops, I failed at that. Therefore, I am a failure . . . Yes, he loves me. Therefore, I am lovable. Oops, now he hates me. Therefore, I am unlovable."

It's essential to explore this way of thinking. It is a potent misunderstanding creating the majority of emotional pain and suffering. But you can release the heightened emotional charge when you embrace these three tips to mastering the new perceptions of your mystic's eye.

You're a Mosaic, Not a Melting Pot

When I was a student at the Institute for Creative Development in Seattle, the founder, Dr. Charles Johnston, reminded us that America originally embraced the notion of being a melting pot. This metaphor led to the belief that we could melt away our differences and become one nation—indivisible. We naïvely believed this would translate into no divisions between us—no notable distinctions. Unfortunately, a melting pot of people wasn't the best image. A mosaic offers a more workable representation, as it can embrace all the possible variations on the theme of being human.

Without fail, Maggie focused on her flaws and limitations; then she beat herself up for not being a better person. She wanted to be a melting pot, where all her inner conflicts merged into one perfect woman—not a mosaic, with lots of different parts. Her unconscious goal of perfection (no flaws or limitations) simply wasn't reachable. Consciously, Maggie knew no one could be perfect, but this kind of conscious awareness doesn't change unconscious patterns.

Weaknesses are not a statement about who you are.

This notion that she could be without flaws was a big misunderstanding. One day after she presented a litany of her shortcomings and failures, I said, "You know, Maggie, you're not designed to be monochromatic. You can't be just the color of goodness, love, kindness, or pure positivity in action. That's what you've been learning here. Life, as we are destined to experience it, is the tension between opposites."

Maggie slowly nodded her head. The tears began flowing once again. This was a very emotional awakening for Maggie, but the strength of her courage and tenacity kept her going. I was quiet for a moment, waiting for her to speak; instead, she gestured me to go on.

"Think of yourself as a mosaic, Maggie—a picture composed of small pieces of colored stone or tile. Have you ever run your hand over a mosaic? It has a bumpy smoothness reflecting all the various shapes and sizes of its components. Every piece adds to the whole mosaic—creating a textured feel that can include smooth, rough, flat, uneven, rounded, and so on. No piece by itself is the mosaic. The mosaic requires all its pieces to be complete."

Maggie's voice squeaked a bit as she said, "Oh my god. How I would love for that to be true about me! To even imagine I might be okay—even if I have parts of me that are broken—is a bit overwhelming."

_____
You are designed to be a mosaic.
_____

No one experience—strength *or* weakness—is capable of reflecting who you are in your totality! It can only reflect an aspect—or, from your new perspective, an experience that arises and then passes away. To claim any strength or weakness as your identity is like pointing to one or two of the stones in the mosaic and saying that's the whole work of art!

None of these experiences on the loop—whether strength or weakness—can reflect the total you. Why? The energy shaping the experiences keeps moving. Like a silent shape-shifter, the life force breathing you alive, moment to moment, keeps flowing from one position into another.

Check it out for yourself. The flow of life isn't a metaphor or a cute New Age tagline. It's a verifiable reality even closer than your breath. Like an enchanted kaleidoscope, it keeps rearranging itself into an infinite array of new patterns.

All Experiences Are Valid and Incomplete

When Max heard this piece of the wisdom of his discontent, he said, "That notion gives me a powerful sense of release. If every experience is only a single point on my infinity loop, it doesn't make sense to hang on to any of them as me."

When these single points are landmarks, they each have a valid perception. It reflects the only view possible from that specific position; it's the point from which the view is being seen; it provides the literal viewpoint for each strength and weakness.

But that's not all. No matter how real or true the experience feels or the perception looks, it can never be the whole truth. The view will always be incomplete in terms of the whole picture. Each view can offer only a part of the information available to help you make a good decision.

Max summed it up this way: "So every single perception and experience I have is valid because it reflects the only view possible from that certain point?" He paused for confirmation. I nodded, and he continued, "So you can't say it's accurate as in 'the correct view' because that particular view is incomplete in terms of the whole picture by virtue of the fact that it's just one viewpoint, right?"

Every experience on the infinity loop is both valid and incomplete.

Max put his finger right on the button. Let me recap the practical and smart application of that information (remember that's our definition of wisdom): No matter what you're experiencing—strength or weakness—it can't be a reflection of who you are in your totality! Claiming it to be so is like pointing to that one bit of tile in the mosaic—regardless of whether it's beautiful or ugly—and saying that's the whole piece!

Who You Are Is More Than You Think

It is much easier to move all the way around the loop graciously and comfortably when you realize your emotions are *not* statements about who you are, nor are they necessarily calls to action.

When you realize emotions are not statements about your identity, value, or worth as a person, you become more open to reflect. You can watch the emotional reaction—minus its heightened emotional charge—arise and pass away in your body and mind. Remember, who you are is much more than the up-and-down rhythm of emotional life.

The Rhythm of Your Emotional Body

When you understand the rhythm of life's flow, you can manage the rhythm of your emotional life. Let's imagine you have an emotional body as well as your physical one, but the emotional body is invisible.

Although you probably can't see it (unless you're a gifted psychic), as you journey around your loop, you can definitely feel your emotional body responding. It registers pleasant feeling, unpleasant feeling, and, as is the case much of the time, neutrality or not feeling much, one way or the other.

You can learn the rhythm of your emotional body. Endlessly, it is carried back and forth between the opposites that make up your polar pair—lifting you up and down, and then up and down—over and over.

Life's rhythms and the rhythms of your emotional body are knowable; they are available to you. Flowing with these rhythms includes relaxing into your resistance as you move from one pole to its opposite. Going with the flow does *not* mean having no resistance at all. Remember the guidance from our mystic friend, Ta Hui: "Real harmony is neither to go with nor to go against. Instead, let reality possess you."

The wisdom of your discontent tells you that the important reality here is the rhythm of life, flowing between opposites. This is the key to becoming unflappable. Then Ta Hui tells you what to do. He gives you a strategy, or a way to respond to your situation: "Just allow yourself to be overwhelmed by the inescapable flow between opposites and you will find immense peace."

The Emergence of a Paradoxical Peace

When you take a position on a controversial topic—whether you're for or against—simply accept it. By recognizing your stance, you are freed from letting it define who you are. Just allow your experience—whatever it is. Watch it. Accept it for what it is—an emotional reaction—no matter how well thought out. And with the help of this work and some mindfulness, you'll have what you need to move from reaction to reflection.

Going with the flow includes relaxing into your resistance.

This kind of peace is a paradox because it allows you to bring the things that make you unhappy into your picture of a happy time. Your acceptance of what is doesn't prevent you from taking action to change it. It's not a passive peace; it's a paradoxical peace. If someone is attacking you, fight for your life. If someone is trying to manipulate you, protect yourself. If you see that someone is hungry, feed her. But you know your deepest or biggest identity is not a fighter, protector, or provider.

When you can see with both your mystic's eye and your mind's eye, you naturally live in harmony with our paradoxical world. This mysterious way of perceiving fills you with more information and greater compassion—for yourself and others.

Looking confused, Maggie asked me to explain what I meant. I pulled out this picture to demonstrate.

The Old Woman and the Young Girl

hag or beautiful girl?

To demonstrate my point about perspective shifts, I asked Maggie to look at the image above and tell me who she saw first, the old woman or the young girl. Confused, she said, "I only see an old woman. There isn't any young girl." I encouraged her to keep looking. Finally, she exclaimed, "There she is! But now I can't see the old woman."

How can this picture be both an old woman and a young beautiful girl? Doesn't it have to be either one or the other? Not when they are both made up of the same lines.

There is no separation between the old woman and the young girl because each is defined by the other. One doesn't exist without the other. They are in fact interdependent and complementary. Sound familiar?

A well-developed mystic's eye can see both at the same time. When you can't access this kind of perception, just remember the paradox is real and is there—whether you can see it or not. It's just like how you relate to the sun on a cloudy day; you know it's still there even though it's out of sight.

To see both the old woman and the young girl simultaneously requires a third neural pathway in the brain. First you have to see one of them—and then the other. Then watch them change back and forth. With practice, you can catch them happening simultaneously. Logically, you can't see them both at once, because the two images are made out of the same lines—yet, it's possible. So you meet another valuable use for the notion of paradox—explaining the unexplainable.

The more you practice going back and forth between the two images, the more likely you'll eventually see them simultaneously. But whether you can or you can't, you now know they are both there—and inseparable.

Clearing the Interference

You're now privy to the only interference that is really relevant to finding inner peace—the heightened emotional charge—and whether you have enough awareness to spot it when it appears. For now, let's assume you are aware of this heightened emotional charge. Let's go through the steps of how to clear it—quickly, easily, simply. Take another look at those interferences you marked on the loop. Let's take just one of them first.

Preparing to Clear Your Interference

- Place your attention where you experience the resistance happening in your body.

- Notice where you feel the resistance in your body: Is it in your head, jaw, eyes, neck, shoulders, arms, chest, stomach, intestines, hips, back, legs, or feet?

- Notice the sensations that make up the resistance: Is it hot or cold; warm or cool; icy or fiery; numb or stinging; moving or stationary; prickly or taut; light or dark; circular, square, or oblong; silent or noisy?

- Are there any images of people or objects that show up with the sensations? Notice the details of these images. For example, are they in black and white or in color; are they close to you or distant; are they big or small?

- Are there sounds? Notice their characteristics: loud or soft, distant or close, melodious or noisy, rhythmic or discordant.

Questions to Clear Your Interference

While you focus on this experience, contemplate these questions:

- *What if this experience is only a waning of my strengths?* Notice what happens in your body as you open to this possibility.

- *What if this experience is a signal that it's time to rebalance, renew, and expand?* Notice what happens in your body as you allow this experience to give you guidance for navigating the rhythms of life and your emotional body.

- *What if this experience is not, in any way, a statement about my identity; who I am; or my value, worth, or goodness as a person?* Notice what happens in your body as you reflect on the possibility that this is true.

By this time, your body will feel considerably different. Much, if not all, of the resistance will be gone. These questions work much like a magical stain remover that takes that red wine you spilled on your carpet and makes it disappear. Recalling the experience, or thinking its name, will now produce a different response.

All Clear?

Do you now feel a willingness in your mind and body to be present to this experience as it arises and passes away in your journey around the infinity loop?

If there is still a lingering emotional charge, please see the Resources section for how to remove it, or address it in Step Six. There, you'll learn about accessing the Larger Living System as an additional tool. If your emotional charge is still very high after that process, it means you need to seek additional support and guidance to unravel this particular knot.

If there is more than one Unresolvable Dilemma at play in your scenario, identify them and work with each one individually. This way you will achieve the clarity and emotional calm you want in the situation or circumstance you're working with. If there is unresolved trauma from past events, I recommend seeing a trauma therapist to clear the past event, freeing you to move forward unencumbered by your history.

You may never come to like the experience, and you may never look forward to having it again, but you're now free to perceive it as simply an experience that is yours to explore. It's not personal to you. It's just a landmark that you frequently have to pass as you travel through this particular Unresolvable Dilemma with less anxiety and angst.

Now that you know the process, take each landmark you starred and run it through these three alternative views:

1. What if this experience is only a waning of my strengths?

2. What if this experience is a signal that it's time to rebalance, renew, and expand?

3. What if this experience is not, in any way, a statement about my identity; who I am; or my value, worth, or goodness as a person?

Notice how each landmark feels in your body *before* and *after* you use these three new perceptions. The difference should be noticeable.

Assuming your body now feels much less stressed in the presence of those unwanted experiences, this is the telling moment. How did you do? Do you feel more at peace with all the experiences you identified in Step One as part of your Unresolvable Dilemma? Let's find out.

Are You There Yet?

Let's do an experiment to see if your unconscious mind is willing to accept this wisdom of your discontent and make it your own.

A note for the skeptical and cynical parts of you: this experiment may seem a little out there, but it's how you infuse the change into your brain and body so it's easier to access. Once again, suspend any disbelief and imagine as if the following really can occur. Let's do it now!

Tracing the Infinity Loop

1. Look at your completed infinity loop and place your index finger on the center point where the two loops meet.

2. Move your finger slowly, pressing it lightly against the paper. Follow the shape of the infinity loop and move in the direction of the flow: one pole's strengths to its own weaknesses, to the opposite pole's strengths to its own weaknesses, and back to the opposite pole's strengths.

3. As you slowly move your index finger around the infinity loop, heighten the feeling of the strengths and weaknesses in your body as you meet them. Feel each emotion as fully as you can. Whenever your finger starts to stick to the paper or to jump over areas, stop! This is a signal from your unconscious mind that it has not yet fully incorporated the three alternative viewpoints you've just learned.

4. Be kind to your unconscious mind and take a moment. Notice the experiences you were focused on when your finger stuck to the paper or jumped over some space on the loop.

5. Once again, run each of those experiences through the three alternate viewpoints, as you did earlier. Check your body for any of that lingering emotional charge.

6. Now try moving your finger again. If your finger got stuck, will it now move?

7. If your finger leaped over a particular spot, is it now able to keep contact with the loop in that area?

8. When you can run your index finger easily all the way around your infinity loop, and your body feels at ease, you know your unconscious mind has no more strong objections to this new option of response.

This is great! You've got 80 percent of the job done. (The other 20 percent is in Step Six.) The objections or concerns are no longer of any major significance. You've got a green light for embracing the two opposites rather than choosing one over the other.

Maggie and Max

When I explained the tracing of the infinity loop part of Step Five to Maggie and Max, they both looked at me like I was crazy. They called it flaky, and neither of them was comfortable with it.

Max said, "I'll do it, but just don't tell anyone, okay?" He was totally surprised when his finger kept sticking over the strengths of failure and the weaknesses of success. But he went back and ran through the three alternative views once again and to his delight and surprise, his finger stopped sticking and was able to move on. Wide-eyed, he once again grinned and said, "Well, I'll be darned. Good stuff, but definitely odd."

Maggie asked, "Do I have to do this finger thing? I feel silly."

I said, "Don't you want to know if all you've done so far has made a difference?" She sighed and put her finger on the loop. It kept getting stuck, so she repeatedly ran the troublesome landmarks through the three alternative views. After about three minutes, her finger sailed smoothly around the complete loop, without out a hitch. She looked at me and simply smiled.

You've started developing a knack for relaxing into your emotional flow, whether that flow feels open, closed, resistant, pleasant, unpleasant, or neutral. This creates presence, matures your emotional intelligence, and expands your conscious awareness. It grants you a sense of peace and calm in the midst of life's emotional turmoil—in other words, you start experiencing the surprising delight of being unflappable.

The Big Finale: Step Six

Now it's time for the grand culmination of your efforts! Step Six shows you how to take the wisdom of your discontent and install it into your brain and body. Once your brain's neurons have a coding for this perceptual knack, you have a new neural pathway available. It offers the unconscious mind the option of perceiving life as either a both/and adventure, or an either/or predicament.

Expanding your brain's neural network means you can manage your Unresolvable Dilemma without working so hard to make it happen! You finally have your unconscious mind on your side.

16
STEP SIX—ENJOYING THE RIDE

TOOLS YOU'LL NEED FOR STEP SIX

*Your **willingness, intention, conviction, doubt,** and **connection to a larger system:** to experience the ride and go with the flow in your body-mind*

Now that you know what the Land of Unresolvable Dilemma is, have explored its terrain, and learned how to navigate its ups and downs and twists and turns, it's time to put it all together.

Remember when I said you have to have more awareness than negative emotion? Now you need to ramp up your awareness so you can use these new perspectives with maximum effectiveness. You can do this fairly easily. Just access your relationship with the Larger Living System—or imagine as if you have a relationship, and that it's a good one! In Part One you received a list of what to bring with you on this trip, and you've seen them mentioned in every step so far. To enjoy the ride, be certain you pull these three in particular out of your bag: your willingness, conviction, and connection to a larger system.

HERE'S WHAT WE'RE GOING TO DO IN STEP SIX

1. Get distance as you place your infinity loop map on the floor

2. Ask, Is the universe a friendly place?

3. Connect as you link to the Larger Living System and Three-Point Balancing Act

4. Integrate as you walk around the map of your infinity loop

5. Get an image of your new relationship with your dilemma

6. Test your body's experience as the evidence of new neural pathways and success

If you don't feel you have a connection, or if you believe you do but can't really feel it in your body, try this: Imagine as if you are willing to be convinced that you are connected to that Larger Living System called God, Mystery, the Light, Suchness, Christ Consciousness, and a hundred other names. That's it. There's nothing more.

Why is this necessary? You've just encountered the possibility that you're not who you thought you were—not really. Most folks get a bit skittish when they encounter the notion that they're neither their weaknesses *nor* their strengths. The most common question then becomes, Well if the strengths and weaknesses aren't who I am, then who am I? In the Land of Unresolvable Dilemma, you can't just fix the problem or ignore this question. You have to find the polar pair at the root of the confusion.

That question brings spirituality into the game. Suddenly you want answers about the notions of spirit and soul, and the Divine Itself. These are questions to answer in your own way and in your own time. But for the purposes of your work here, imagining you are part of a Larger Living System is all you need to do. This simple act adequately ramps up your awareness that a larger picture is possible.

Your Divine Self and Your Human Self

Reluctantly, Max revealed that when he took a breath and looked upward, his quest for success seemed small in comparison to the larger quests of the world—like eradicating poverty, hunger, war, domestic violence, murder, and mayhem. He wondered where he fit in the larger scheme.

Maggie, however, contemplated questions of purpose and meaning almost daily. She desperately wanted to believe in something greater than herself—and better than herself. But her conviction that God found her unseemly and unworthy made connecting with that greater reality difficult.

Since we blew a hole in that old sense of identity based on your strengths and weaknesses, you need something else to stand on in the interim. So you're going to step into a larger and more expanded sense of identity—a deeper and wider sense of yourself that includes not just your human self (personality) but also your divine self (essence).

Here's what I mean by divine self or essence. You can take a pot of liquid gold and make it into earrings, bracelets, watches, necklaces, rings, tie tacks, and so forth. But regardless of the varying shapes, the essence of each item remains gold—intact and unchanged by the shape it becomes. Your essence is that gold. Your personality is the shape the gold has taken. It can be scratched, or it can be smooth. It can be broken or intact, beautiful or ugly. The important thing to remember is that, essentially, your personality is made of gold.

What is this divine gold? God? Light? The Mystery? Consciousness? Buddha Nature? Awareness? Whatever language you use, imagine yourself *convinced*—if only for just a moment—that it is true. You really are *human at your circumference and divine at your core.*

Now imagine you believe you are an important and necessary part of that Larger Living System—regardless of how you name it. Honor your skepticism or cynicism, and then suspend your disbelief. Think: *I am an important and necessary part of that Larger Living System.* Envision it. Hear it. Feel it. Taste it. Smell it.

Imagine you are *essential* to the Larger Living System, connected to it, needed by it, inseparable from it, and completely accepted by it—as you are—without changing a single thing. The sky embraces the stars and the moon as they are, without question. Doesn't life embrace and accept you, as you are, with every breath?

The Alchemical Nature of Faith

In the Land of Unresolvable Dilemma, faith is essential. In one of his books, Don Miguel Ruiz, a modern mystic from the Toltec tradition, points out that we are all born with faith. However, we place this precious gift into the hands of untruths. We become quite faithful to our beliefs that we are bad, stupid, inadequate, deficient, ugly, unlovable, failures, and so on. Faith does its job—regardless of where you put it, so this tendency to misplace faith has a negative effect. Instead, you can put your faith in Life, in the Whole, in the wonder of things, in yourself as a part of the Whole—these make up the fertile soil where faith takes root and blossoms in your daily life.

Faith provides food for your soul. It quenches your spirit's thirst for a taste of home. It offers hope for the heart and wisdom for the mind. It is undeniable that Life is mysterious. When you put your faith in that mystery, it changes everything.

Faith can change your perception of the personality so it becomes transparent and reveals its golden essence. This Mystery *is* you, and lives life *through* you (and all other things)—including your thoughts, feelings, and personality. When you experience this Mystery as paradoxically both you and not you, great peace, joy, and love naturally arise—and the incredible wonder of being unflappable.

A Spiritual Experience

Everyone I meet has had some kind of spiritual experience. I define a spiritual experience as one that you can't describe—it takes your breath away, leaves you speechless, strikes you mute with awe.

Here are a few examples of spiritual experiences that people have shared with me over the years:

- Giving birth
- Watching a baby being born
- Seeing a field of wheat waving in the wind
- Hearing the call of a loon
- Listening to the rat-tat-tat of a woodpecker
- Seeing roiling ocean waves during a winter storm
- Gazing at the aurora borealis
- Witnessing a lunar or solar eclipse
- Gardening and feeling that your hands belong to the earth
- Plucking fresh fruit from a tree and savoring its juice
- Hearing the wind rustle the leaves of the trees
- Watching a mesmerizing live theatre performance
- Hearing the encompassing sound of a live symphonic orchestra
- Looking in your partner's eyes and feeling a love that has no words
- Spotting a bald eagle as it soars
- Watching the graceful elegance of a lion as it awakens and stretches its body out of a lazy sleep
- Catching sight of a blue heron on a city dock, poised and still as a statue
- Glimpsing that rare rainbow encircling the moon with kaleidoscopic hues
- Sitting on a mountaintop with silence and stillness as your only companions.

Take a moment to connect with some of your own spiritual experiences. You have them—everyone does—but you may not have realized what they were.

Bigger than Yourself

Spiritual experiences expand your sense of identity. They blur your ability to distinguish between yourself and others, allowing a felt sense of that Oneness we talked about earlier. You automatically become aware that you are part of something larger than yourself. You automatically become bigger than your dilemma, bigger than your problems, bigger than your normal sense of self as a small and limited, albeit wonderful, personality. When this occurs, you become free to embrace your dilemma rather than trapped into fighting it.

The Three-Point Balancing Act

Now it's time to try out that Three-Point Balancing Act you read about in Part One. This means taking the stance that gives you emotional stability by making you bigger than the Unresolvable Dilemma and connecting you to the perceptions of your mystic's eye. This creates the environment for managing any situation from a balanced position—and for navigating the Land of Unresolvable Dilemma with ease, presence, and grace.

Remember, this is done by embracing both dimensions of your being:

- Two of the three points are focused on your humanity (with its mind's eye) in the world of opposites, feeling life fully as it moves through your body.

- The remaining point is focused on your divinity (with its mystic's eye) perceiving the harmony of this ongoing, creative, dynamic tension between polar pairs.

Does this seem illogical? Correct. Nonetheless, it is possible—thanks to our mysterious paradoxical nature.

The Three-Point Balancing Act gives you all you need to understand and accept the ongoing creative dynamic tension of life. It becomes yours to explore and experience, rather than to grasp or avoid. And you can see the journey itself, whether it's easy or hard, is not a statement about who you are.

Once Max discovered he did believe in something larger than himself—and that he could remember experiencing something that made him feel simultaneously relaxed and awesome—he was chomping at the bit to do Step Six. He was happy to contemplate his identity as something other than strengths and weaknesses. He shared that he had been a closeted flower child for years and had tried what seemed like every personal-growth seminar possible.

But Max still had a little trouble with this notion of the Three-Point Balancing Act. It all seemed a bit obtuse to him. He said he needed something more concrete. To help him get a better handle on the notion, I showed him an exercise I call Getting Behind the Chair.

Getting Behind the Chair

1. Sit down in a chair and feel the inner tug-of-war you're working with in your body.

2. Imagine as if you can leave your body-mind struggling with that Unresolvable Dilemma in the chair, and stand up.

3. Position yourself physically behind your chair as if stepping into your divine self/spiritual connection with the Larger Living System.

4. Imagine as if you can see your body-mind (personality/human self) still sitting in the chair in front of you struggling with the dilemma.

5. In the standing position, extend your hands and arms outward as if you're embracing the you sitting in the chair who must, *by design*, endure this inner tug-of-war.

6. Experience what it's like to have access to both your human and spiritual perspectives simultaneously.

7. Relax and allow the wisdom of your discontent to infuse your body-mind system, allowing a new sense of peace and calm.

I asked Max to think of his struggle with success versus failure and to really feel whatever was left of the tug-of-war in his body. When he had the feeling, I had him imagine his body (and its struggle with the dilemma) staying in the chair as he literally got up and stood behind the chair. He could visualize himself sitting in the chair easily. If you can't, just imagine as if you could see or sense yourself (your body-mind) sitting in the chair and feeling that inner tug-of-war. If you can't actually get up, just imagine as if you're standing behind the chair as well.

Then I had Max hold out his hands as if embracing his imagined body sitting in the chair in front of him, struggling with the dilemma. Max did this and nodded, saying, "Okay, I get it. These are the two dimensions happening at the same time. There's my personality and body-mind down there in front of me. And then my divine self with this Larger Living System perspective behind that lets me see the bigger picture. I'm both of these perspectives happening simultaneously. I couldn't see this unless I got behind the chair."

About three months later, Max shared the following: "You remember that Getting Behind the Chair thing you showed me?" I nodded. "Well," he continued, "I've been using that maybe three or four times a day since then, and I have to tell you, it's really helped me a lot. I don't even need to stand up. I just imagine I am. It's an absolute paradox, but it's really making a difference in how I'm seeing myself and my life."

Many students report that this exercise has become a daily reminder of doing the entire Six-Step Process. Give it a try to get a clearer sense of the Three-Point Balancing Act:

- Two of the three points are solidly placed in the world of duality or opposites. Remember the feet on both edges of the loop.

- The remaining point is solidly placed in the world of Spirit, the Divine, God, the Mystery, and so on.

This is a simple guide for how to follow the advice of Jesus when he said, "Be in the world, but not of the world." Think he might have been giving us a clue for navigating the Land of Unresolvable Dilemma?

A Friendly Universe?

Maggie was still uncomfortable with the notion of God. When she rejected her fundamentalist upbringing, her emotional recoil from anything even slightly similar remained. She liked the idea of a Larger Living System, but she still grappled with a few big questions.

She had many spiritual experiences, but she didn't trust they meant anything. Because she was such a thinker, I brought Einstein into the conversation by sharing one of his most famous questions: "Is the universe a friendly place?"

"Well," said Maggie, "that depends on how you define *friendly*."

If *friendly* means the universe is "always kind and considerate and safe to be with," then clearly you have to answer no. But what if we altered our definition of *friendly* to mean "available for support, guidance, balance, renewal, and growth"? Wouldn't that be a completely different perspective on the place we live?

Contemplate your own definition of *friendly*, and see how it affects your answer. Your mystic's eye reveals our world is a world of opposites, flowing back and forth between each other. That means kindness comes with cruelty, consideration comes with neglect, and safety comes with risk.

So here's the paradox: Your mind's eye sets up what you like against what you dislike and perceives the Larger System as dangerous, unsafe, and unfriendly. Your mystic's eye embraces opposites and the paradoxical nature of being human and perceives the Larger System as friendly, challenging, and willing to help you grow in all the ways it can.

When I asked Maggie to connect with this Larger Living System, she withdrew, embarrassed. With tears in her eyes, she shared, "I'm just too broken. It's not possible for me to be accepted in a friendly universe—and if I am, I don't know if I can handle it. It's too . . . too . . . overwhelming."

After a few minutes, she recovered and said, "But I'm going to try it anyway; even though I'm scared." That was Maggie's spirit, in a nutshell: committed, dedicated, and stubborn.

As for Max, he found the existence of a friendly universe through his work. He explained: "When I step out from behind the proscenium onto the stage, something happens. I somehow step out of my made-up self into what I feel is the real me. There's space there and lightness, and I don't have to think about what I'm doing. It just happens. I don't talk about this much—it sounds stupid and too la-la land—but the fact is, I love just being me!" He gave a little laugh of embarrassment and continued on. "I forget about everything else: what the audience is going to think of me, what the guys who hired me will think—even my own self-criticism falls into silence. There's just this space, and we're like one thing. I'm never more relaxed than when I'm presenting in front of a large audience."

Walking Infinity

Now that you have your connection to the Larger Living System, you're ready to integrate all you've learned into your brain and body. You're going to physically walk on your infinity loop. This guides your brain and body to lay down the exact neural pathways to turn the wisdom of your discontent into *your* wisdom, easily accessible and easily useable, freeing you to enter the world of the Marketplace Mystic and the joys of being unflappable.

Walking Infinity with Maggie

I asked Maggie to imagine that her infinity loop lay out on the floor in front of her. (It's also fine to use yarn or string, or the loop you've already drawn. However, because our goal is the installation of this wisdom into your brain, it's most efficient to just imagine it out there in front of you. When you use objects, it supports a passive stance for the unconscious mind. When you insist on imagination, you give the unconscious mind a kick in the pants and force it to become actively involved and use abilities that may be lying dormant.)

Even though Maggie was very good at visualizing her personal tragedies, romantic and otherwise, she claimed incompetence at conjuring up this image. Not a problem. I gave her three crayons—red, blue, and yellow. She marked the middle of the infinity loop with one of them and used the remaining two to mark the outside edge of each of the two loops of the symbol. Her mind naturally filled in the rest of the loop.

I told her to point out which loop held which opposite. She pointed to the left loop as fulfilling her own needs and to the right loop as fulfilling others' needs.

Needs of Professional and Personal Life

Strengths

happiness, creativity, fulfillment, satisfaction, joy, meaning, purpose, sense of belonging, connection, optimism, drive, single-mindedness, vision, insight, motivation, self-acceptance, participation in life, gratitude, recognition, pleasure, time for reflection, awareness

Strengths

love, joy, happiness, fulfillment, success, connection, creativity, community, belonging, satisfaction, contribution, laughter, humor, a wider perspective, curiosity, amazement, diversity, wonder, challenge, pleasure, approval, appreciation, accomplishment

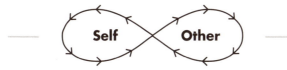

Weaknesses

guilt, selfishness, hell, isolation, greed, huge ego, narcissism, self-importance, self-indulgence, arrogance, cockiness, egotism, haughtiness, being too big for your britches, pride, overconfidence, being a bad person, ugliness, cruelty, unkindness, unfriendliness

Weaknesses

exhaustion, irritation, resentment, anger, pessimism, depression, despair, unhappiness, joylessness, apathy, frustration, hopelessness, doom, indifference, laziness, meaninglessness, purposelessness, feeling lost, disappearance, abandonment, bitterness

I guided her to step onto the middle point of the infinity loop and to notice what she felt in her body—just as she had when we first began. Was she pulled toward one? Repelled by the other?

She said, "I still feel really pulled toward my own needs and repelled by others' needs. Is that okay? I thought it might be different now."

I explained that our preceding conversations had answered all her objections and concerns about the *possibility* of changing her response to this dilemma. If we hadn't been successful, her unconscious mind wouldn't have allowed us to reach Step Six. Now that we're here, it means we have a clear go signal from the unconscious to proceed and actually *make the change.*

I directed Maggie to step back off the loop and to take a moment to imagine her connection with the Larger Living System—her newfound possibility of a Friendly Universe. I reminded her to imagine as if she had the courage, willingness, and conviction to reach out and discover a gracious, responsive, and welcoming universe—completely willing to support her right here and now. It would be larger than her and full of all the support and lovingkindness she could ever dream of.

She closed her eyes and took a deep breath. Then she raised her hands and extended them with the palms open and facing upward. After a minute or so, she said, "Okay, I'm connected." I asked if she could feel it in her body. She replied, "Yes—and I never thought anything could feel so wonderful!" Sure enough—a small tear slipped out of her eye and gently rolled down her cheek.

In a quiet voice, I explained what I wanted her to do next.

"Okay, Maggie, now you're ready to walk around the infinity loop, exploring your polar pair in the Land of Unresolvable Dilemma, and how it feels to allow each experience. Allow every landmark you know is there to simply be there. Thoroughly enjoy the strengths and recognize the unpleasant weaknesses as signals that it's time to let go of where you've been and to move on to the opposite. Your system wants to rebalance, renew, and expand. But I want you to stay connected with the Larger System while you do this—as if your connection lives in your breath or your heartbeat, as if it's something you can't get away from."

She nodded in agreement. I continued. "In addition, while you're walking, I want you to say out loud, so you can hear it, these words—*I can allow both my needs and the needs of others. Neither is a statement about who I am.* If saying 'neither is a statement about who I am' doesn't feel right for you, you can say 'I am both of these and more.' The first is a more Zen approach, finding who you are by elimination. The second is a more Sufi approach, finding who you are by embracing everything. Keep repeating your phrase as you walk the loop. Do you have any questions? Is there anything you need to say or do before you begin this walk?"

She shook her head and began. She moved from the strengths of the *Other* pole down into its own weaknesses, then up to the strengths of the *Self* pole and then down into its own weaknesses.

As she walked, I talked to her unconscious mind. I'm including what I said so you can read it for yourself (or have a friend read it to you) when you're walking around your loop. You don't have to read it every time you walk your infinity loop, just once or twice to get the hang of it and to give your unconscious mind the guidance and direction it needs to integrate this process into your brain.

Here is the hypnotic language, purposefully including the incorrect grammar that makes hypnosis highly effective. Remember, this is for your unconscious mind, not your conscious one.

As you're walking infinity, go ahead now . . . allow and accept each experience as you meet it along the way . . . feel it fully in your body . . . just breathing into its presence and allowing it to be there . . . that's right . . . and just staying connected . . . in your own way . . . feel your highest sense of expanded self . . . that you are larger than your dilemma . . . remembering you are not these experiences . . . you are so much more . . . allow your Larger Self to simply experience the experience . . . be like the sky behind the clouds . . . feel the presence of the clouds moving by . . . yet be neither for the clouds nor against them . . . be like the ocean beneath the waves moving on the surface . . . still in your depths . . . freeing the waves to be there in their own way . . .

That's right . . . notice how those strengths dissolve into what you have learned to call weaknesses . . . notice those weaknesses . . . as unpleasant as those signals may be . . . naturally moving you toward . . . and taking on the shape of . . . those strengths of that seemingly opposite pole . . . become more and more aware as you move in that infinite rhythm of life . . . how these two things that had seemed so opposed . . . are now . . . and always have been . . . in a deep harmony . . . discover that rhythm that is the rhythm . . . of this dance of opposites . . . unfolding again and again . . . as you walk with this rhythm . . . feeling it fully . . . yet knowing these strengths and weaknesses are not who you are . . . for you are . . . in reality . . . so much more.

I directed Maggie to continue walking until she could move with ease through all the strengths and weaknesses of each pole. When that happened, she was to come to the center point again and stop. She walked around the loop for another minute or so before she became motionless at the center.

She whispered, "I feel so different, so balanced and quiet. It's wonderful." I asked her to allow an image or a symbol to arise in her mind representing this new experience, something she could keep with her and draw upon now and throughout the future. Her image was an infinity loop pulsing in her heart. It had golden threads flowing outward toward others and simultaneously curving back to embrace her from head to toe—very beautiful.

To be certain we had succeeded in our quest to change her emotional response to the dilemma, I asked Maggie to check her body. Did it feel different now? Was she still pulled toward the *Self* pole and away from the *Other* pole? Or vice versa? Was she more neutral now?

She turned her attention inward and then shared, "You know, I just feel I can do it now. I don't feel that strongly about either one. Right now, it just seems like something I can manage—first me, then them, then me, then them. There's a rhythm to it that I wasn't aware of before. It's very cool!"

I had Maggie pick up her imaginary loop from the floor and put it in her pocket. Anytime she needed it, she could just pull it out and start the Six Steps.

Walking Infinity with Max

When it was time for Max to walk around his infinity loop of success and failure, he had a much harder time than Maggie did. He could conjure up the notion of a Larger Living System, but he had trouble feeling it in his body.

Achievement

Strengths

achievement, praise, recognition, accolades, appreciation, wealth, happiness, enjoyment, satisfaction, self-esteem, pride, accomplishment, approval, love, respect, attention, kindness, colleagues, triumph, name recognition, fulfillment, contentment, gratitude, acknowledgment

Strengths

challenge, opportunity, learning, growth, re-examination, creativity, options, change of direction, new focus, exploration, adventure, more education, fresh beginnings, evolution, development, imagination, resourcefulness, innovation, originality, inspiration, motivation

Weaknesses

exhaustion, irritability, short temper, harshness, insensitivity to others, prickliness, rudeness, arrogance, egotism, severity, manipulation, difficulty, impatience, being controlling, low energy, isolation, disconnection, loneliness, unhappiness, confusion

Weaknesses

being a loser, a dud, a has-been, unworthy, nameless, faceless, invisible, and lost; blame; embarrassment; poverty; anonymity; shame; humiliation; mortification; chagrin; fear; terror; anger; rage; self-pity; self-hatred; dread; anxiety; frustration; guilt; sadness

I reminded him of the three places where he'd had a taste of this bigger space: on his boat, when he stepped on stage in front of a large audience, and when he stood behind the chair. As he remembered these events, he began to relax.

These experiences were already coded into his brain. Thinking of them allowed him to re-experience the calm he'd felt on his boat, the lightness and ease of being himself on stage, and the distance that gave him the bigger picture when he'd moved behind the chair. Now he had the notion of a Larger Living System and the feelings in his body to accompany it.

Here's how Max walked infinity. I guided him as I had Maggie. Max was a good visualizer and could easily imagine the infinity loop in front of him on the floor. He checked how his body felt in relation to his dilemma—still pulled toward success and repelled from failure. He connected to his notion of a Larger Living System, and then added in the calm, ease, and lightness that he'd discovered he could pull up in his body.

Then he walked around the loop, in the direction he'd learned, speaking the same words Maggie had said, out loud, but using his polar pair: "I can allow both success and failure. Neither is a statement about who I am." While he walked, I guided his unconscious mind with the same words I'd used with Maggie. He stopped when he felt he could move easily through all his strengths and weaknesses on both loops. Standing in the center point of the loop, he allowed a symbol to arise that would carry the power of his new understanding.

He described his symbol as a silver infinity loop with an image of his wallet on one side and an image of his family on the other; both the wallet and the picture of the family had a smaller infinity loop imposed over them.

With surprise, he said, "I'm a little confused by where this image came from. But the issue of success and failure doesn't seem as important now because there's balance between my work and my family. I'm astonished."

If you remember, Max wanted more time with his family, and it was his fear of failure that kept him from getting it—fear of losing status in his career and fear of the emotions he'd have to deal with if he got closer to his wife and kids.

When he checked how his body felt, he reported a more neutral experience. He wasn't really pulled toward or away from either success or failure. He described a flattening out of his emotional intensity. Once the heightened emotional charge was decreased, the natural balancing had room to fall into place.

Walking Infinity with Ragini

Accessing spiritual experiences was still my biggest challenge. My cynicism disrupted my efforts to create conviction and a connection that seemed truly real. I was willing enough, but it was hard to imagine being connected to something larger than I was that was intrinsically beautiful, positive, and loving.

I discovered how necessary this connection was when I was teaching an NLP course with one of my British colleagues, Roger Vaisey. When the students were busy practicing one of the skills they'd just learned, Roger and I went into a side room and began experimenting with the idea of walking around the infinity loop. Roger wanted me to access my connection with God before we continued.

I scoffed and said, "Come on. We don't need God for this!" Arrogantly, I began walking around the loop by accessing my intellect alone. Within a few seconds, I felt confused, disoriented, and nauseous—I blew out my neural circuits. Roger had to take over teaching for the rest of the day while I went outside, sat with nature, and recovered.

If you have a cynical side like I do, you may want to find something less frilly and poetic than goodness and light to represent the spiritual dimension. The more neutral analogies I previously used in the hypnotic language on pages 201–202 with Maggie work well.

Using these notions to establish my connection, I then walked around my infinity loop for several minutes saying out loud, "I can allow both trust and doubt. Neither is a statement about who I am." As I walked and spoke, I felt the strengths and weaknesses in my body as I navigated each part of the infinity loop.

Faith

Strengths

peace, calm, openness, love, comfort, solace, compassion, honesty, authenticity, facing reality, accepting what is, living in the moment, presence, quiet, joy, letting go, empathy, action, freedom, direction, connection, a part of something larger, belonging

Strengths

inquiry, creativity, re-assessment, challenge, adventure, openness, new options, new direction, freedom, new strategy, openness, willingness, exploration, discovery, fun, excitement, imagination, inspiration, ingenuity, cleverness, motivation, stimulation, fun, involvement

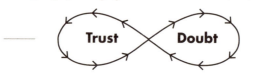

Trust ⋈ **Doubt**

Weaknesses

being a Pollyanna, sugary sweet, saccharine, syrupy, passive, nonthinking, closed to new ideas, and controlling; blind faith; pushiness; anger; judgment; self-righteousness; superiority; pride; denial of reality; illogic; proselytization; insensitivity to others

Weaknesses

being critical, closed, attacking, argumentative, dismissive, sneering, and snide; skepticism; cynicism; judgment; arrogance; sarcasm; coldness; cruelty; unwillingness; defensiveness; rudeness; paralysis; anxiety; despair; hopelessness; fear; panic; helplessness; indecision

When I stopped, the image that came to mind was a see-saw with a child sitting on each end, moving up and down. The see-saw board would hit the ground hard, and the child would laugh as her body lifted up off the board and then plopped back down. She obviously knew how to enjoy the ride and was clearly happy. It actually made me cry. Imagine my little four-year-old self finally fulfilling her desire to find happiness—even when she hit the ground. How sweet is that!

Finally, I checked my body for how it now felt about trust and doubt. Just like Maggie and Max, the heightened emotional charge was gone. There were still some feelings running through my body, but nothing felt significant.

I remember breathing a sigh of great relief. My cynicism was no longer in the driver's seat. Trust and doubt seemed quite fine taking turns driving. They never seem disturbed by my cynic's occasional outbursts from his new position as a backseat driver.

This experience highlights the importance of connecting with the Source. In NLP language, when you go in to change something negative, always take something positive with you that is *equal or greater* in emotional strength and intensity than the negative.

Time to Walk Your Infinity Loop

Now it's your turn. Follow these steps.

1. Imagine your infinity loop out in front of you on the floor. Make it big enough for you to comfortably walk around—at least four or five feet wide if you have the space. Use three markers to outline the shape of the loop if you like, or the loop you've drawn. Determine which loop holds which opposite.

2. Stand in the center and notice in your body how it feels. Are you pulled toward one pole? Repelled by the other? Just notice; don't judge. Step off the loop to just behind the center point.

3. Step into your connection with the Larger Living System— a place connected to your spirit, soul, or essence, allowing you to expand. Feel it, see it, breathe into it. Feel yourself larger than your dilemma—as if you can put out your arms and embrace the situation rather than allowing it to encompass you.

4. Begin walking around the loop, through all the strengths and weaknesses, feeling them as you walk by. As you walk, say out loud, "I can allow both _____ and _____. Neither is a statement about who I am." When you feel you can make the walk with ease, stop.

5. Stand in the center point and notice how you feel: Different? The same? You should feel a distinct absence of the heightened emotional charge. If you still feel a strong lingering emotional charge, go to the energy psychology tools in the Resources section. Once the emotional charge feels adequately reduced, walk the infinity loop again, being sure

to reconnect with your spiritual resource before beginning the walk.

6. Allow an image to arise from within symbolizing all you've learned here. If you wish, make a drawing of it or write a short poem or narrative describing it.

7. Make the final test. Check how you feel in your body now as you contemplate each opposite. Notice that the heightened emotional charge is gone now, no longer of any major significance.

Congratulations! Your brain and body now know what you want them to do in the presence of your Unresolvable Dilemma. You've walked your infinity loop and have a new relationship with your old problem.

The more you walk the loop, think of the loop, and play with opposites every day, the more your brain and body can access your new way of handling Unresolvable Dilemmas. In addition, your brain is already generalizing your new methods and applying them to other predicaments and quandaries. That helps you quickly identify which of those are also Unresolvable Dilemmas and can now be managed.

Now let's conclude with a summary and review of what you've learned and check in with Maggie and Max to see how they're doing a few years into their futures.

CONCLUSION
YOUR NEW WISDOM
IN A NUTSHELL

You now know how to enjoy your ride through the Land of Unresolvable Dilemma. You know how to reduce the amount of time and energy you put into clinging to what you like and avoiding what you dislike. You now have a proven strategy for finding inner peace in daily life gleaned from the psychology of the mystics—those folks whose guidance make life a bit more user-friendly. You know why it's valuable to embrace your discontent. However it arrives, it is a messenger bringing you the gift of this wisdom. You learned that opposites, and thus, Unresolvable Dilemmas, permeate your daily life. And you discovered how your brain normally handles them.

The Old Option: Approach the dilemma as if it were fixable. Fix it by choosing one of the two options as the better choice. Then cling to that choice and avoid, or work to eradicate, the other option. It's an either/or predicament of the mind.

However, you followed the wisdom of your discontent and found a more efficient way to operate in the presence of opposites and Unresolvable Dilemmas. This new way leads to inner peace (cognitive tranquility[12]) and a different brand of happiness (accepting what arises—including your resistance).

The New Option: Approach the predicament as an Unresolvable Dilemma. Manage this by embracing both options as equally important players in a harmonious, complementary partnership. This partnership is dedicated to rebalancing, renewing, and expanding you as a living system—and all those living systems you're a part of. It's a both/and circumstance of your human/divine nature.

The Six-Step Process: A Review

Let's summarize the Six-Step Process for retrieving this wisdom, making it your own, and discovering the knack for being unflappable. If you need more detail, just refer back to each step's chapter to see the list of specific action items.

Step One

The wisdom of your discontent taught you how to create a specific map of your Unresolvable Dilemma's geography—the lay of the land:

1. Use an infinity loop to represent the physical shape of the land.

2. Identify the context, the set of opposites in the dilemma, and the landmarks (strengths and weaknesses) on both sides of the loop.

Step Two

The wisdom of your discontent gave you the secret to traveling safely, efficiently, and most easily through the Land of Unresolvable Dilemma:

1. Stay on the river.

2. Follow its route (from the strengths of one pole to its own weaknesses, to the strengths of the opposite pole and then to its own weaknesses).

3. Honor its hidden pattern of flow between opposites.

4. Be aware of the two paradoxical life forces creating the river's current—the drive to change and the drive to stay the same.

Step Three

The wisdom of your discontent gave you crucial insights into the purpose and function of the Land of Unresolvable Dilemma:

1. Use your mystic's eye to perceive the purpose and function of Unresolvable Dilemma (to rebalance, renew, and expand your life and you).

2. Realize that harmony, inner peace, and that different brand of happiness become yours by recognizing and embracing the never-ending presence of Unresolvable Dilemmas in daily life.

Step Four

The wisdom of your discontent revealed the real culprit causing your suffering in the presence of an Unresolvable Dilemma:

1. Clear the actual interference to going with the flow by reducing the heightened emotional charge attached to the landmarks (strengths and weaknesses), which you starred.

2. Use the key of paradox to manage your emotions by learning how to move from reaction to reflection.

3. Surf the predictable rhythm of your emotional ups and downs—like riding the waves in the ocean.

4. Use this rhythm in creating inner peace and, thus, that different and life-changing brand of happiness you seek.

Step Five

The wisdom of your discontent gave you three alternate ways of perceiving those landmarks you starred on your infinity loop:

1. Use these alternative perceptions (weaknesses are the waning of the strengths; they are signals; they are not statements about your identity) to release the heightened emotional charge.

2. Embrace the situation, circumstance, or emotion as simply an experience to explore.

3. Use your new found freedom to see beyond your personality as defining who you are.

Step Six

The wisdom of your discontent showed you how to install this new way of dealing with Unresolvable Dilemma into your brain and body:

1. Connect with the Larger Living System (using your own language).

2. Unhook your identity from the set of interdependent polar opposites at play.

3. Physically walk your infinity loop.

4. Receive an image from your unconscious mind to use in daily life that represents your new mystical perspective on life as a both/and adventure rather than an either/or predicament.

The Ripple Effect

It's possible you may not do a single thing this book suggests. Even with the best of intentions, projects can slip out of view and slide off to the side. However, merely encountering the notion of Unresolvable Dilemma, complementary opposites, and interdependent polar pairs can change your life forever.

The image of the infinity loop will now trigger your unconscious mind's remembrance of this book. The nudge you've given to your mystic's eye and its ability to perceive things differently will ripple through your unconscious mind, causing a new level of awareness around opposites and the dilemmas they create. The wisdom of your discontent will continue to tap on your shoulder, requesting you embrace its presence and accept its message. As you use the Six-Step Process, you'll find yourself tracing infinity loops in the air and walking them on the ground. Your unconscious mind will begin reshaping your reactions into reflections, and keep you moving toward that gift of inner peace in the presence of your emotional turmoil. What's more, that different and life-changing brand of happiness will start becoming a part of your daily life.

Let's check back with Maggie and Max and see what happened for them a couple of years after they started using this work.

Maggie

Every once in a while, Maggie still comes to see me for what she calls a tune-up. It's usually about some new objection she's uncovered about faith. Or she comes for some reminders about how to get back on the river and regain her ability to manage the Unresolvable Dilemma of self versus other.

Maggie successfully rearranged her life so she could go back to school. In two years, she finished her master's degree in fine arts, specializing in writing. She actually did what she always wanted to do! And she really did learn how to create the balance she'd been seeking: the time to work, enjoy her family and friends, and write essays around her area of professional expertise. Of course, she can still create quite a horrifying tale about her times of imbalance, but now she knows how to relax into her life, not take it too seriously, and let it unfold.

One day she summed up her life this way: "I never thought I could find anything spiritual that would work for me. God and I had just been done for too long. But here I am, risking trust in a Friendly Universe that I have magically started to believe gives me purpose and meaning. It's a mystery how it happened, but I'm so grateful that it did. Life is just better this way—more workable, like you said it would be. And, I'm finally doing what I've always wanted to do. Someday I might even be the writer I think I could be."

Max

Max still comes to see me when he runs into some emotional nuance that throws him back into fear. But he no longer fears failure in his career or his family life. He recovered his sense of passion and purpose in life and consequently started listening to his heart.

He changed the actual direction of his life, taking some mighty big risks for a guy who was once so afraid of them.

Although he loved public speaking, he followed another passion and began a new business using his architectural degree from years before. He'd always loved using his hands, so he decided to use all his skills to do what he loved the most—build. Now Max has gone green, renovating old buildings to bring their inherent energy and usefulness back to life. He says he feels more alive and happy than ever before, and he continues to use the infinity loop to help him stay balanced and keep on track.

Max always described our work together as good coaching. The last time I saw him, he shared these sentiments: "I never believed I had a future. But now I realize a negative future was actually all I ever thought about. Now I believe I have a future, but instead of worrying about it, I seem to just be living my life, doing what needs to be done and trusting that I can, and will, succeed. It's a very different way of living. And as long as I keep that infinity loop with me, I don't seem to feel so lost anymore. It's like a compass that keeps me heading toward home and staying true." Max found his personal proof that the Six-Step Process was indeed an excellent map for navigating the Land of Unresolvable Dilemma.

Ragini

My story, like yours, is still unfolding. My faith continues flowing between trust and doubt, but I now have great confidence in its resilience. Doubt no longer whips me into a frenzy of agonizing marathons run by my mocking skeptic or disparaging cynic. And trust no longer makes me want to throw up, scramble away, and hide from all things sweet, soft, tender, and kind.

Instead, I am more at peace with life, able to embrace its ups and downs, uncertainties, ambiguities, and confusions. Now don't get me wrong—I still feel a desire for certain things I don't have. Envy remains a frequent caller, and I still feel irritation about a few of those things I think I deserve to have and don't. Frustration and irritation are no strangers. But now they're just visitors and not statements about who I am.

I can relax into my human nature (and personality) and let it be. Desires and their accompanying emotions arise and pass away, and I don't have to do anything with them. The freedom to resist what is and still be okay is liberating. The wisdom to simply embrace my resistance makes my life workable. I am both divine and human. I am filled with both gratitude and gripes, making me able to finally enjoy this amazing ride. I can even say I finally found that different and life-changing brand of happiness that knows no opposite. It's not the happiness I thought I was looking for—but I wouldn't trade it for anything.

You

You now have all that you need to verify for yourself that this map is a necessary guide for travel through the Land of Unresolvable Dilemma. Although I am not privy to your personal story, I feel somehow that I am. We are all members of the same species. Your story and mine are in many ways everyone's story. Because you've read this book, I'm assuming the following about you: You have the courage to be yourself—just like the Cowardly Lion in the *The Wizard of Oz*. You have the heart to be your authentic self—just like the Tin Man. You have the brain to find your balanced self—just like the Scarecrow. And because you now know the wicked witch will never fully disappear, you can click your heels together and, like Dorothy, discover there's a way to get back home.

The wisdom of your discontent has always been with you. Dorothy was right. Once you know where to find it, there's no place like home. That home is in your own intelligent mind daring to learn; your own sweet, loving heart daring to be vulnerable and risk feeling truly alive; and your own brilliant spirit, daring to soar beyond the unknown and the known into the unknowable.

With your mystic's eye and a bit of that paradoxical magic, anything is possible—even becoming unflappable. Just embrace the wisdom of your discontent. It won't stop chasing you until you receive its gift and discover how to live life as the both/and adventure it naturally is.

RESOURCES

SOME COMMON UNRESOLVABLE DILEMMAS

Here are 149 common Unresolvable Dilemmas operating in six major areas of daily life. These areas are the places where you have to make decisions, day after day: Relationship, Power, Success, Happiness, Purpose, and Faith. You'll find that many of the dilemmas appear in more than one of these six categories.

Relationship Dilemmas (25):

Dependent versus Independent
Close versus Distant
Self versus Other
My Needs versus Your Needs
Separate versus Connected
Strong versus Weak
Alone versus Together
Right versus Wrong
Love versus Hate
Ally versus Enemy
Free versus Imprisoned
Spontaneous versus Restrained
Dominant versus Submissive
War versus Peace
Better Than versus Less Than

Being Seen versus Being Invisible
Courage versus Cowardice
Man versus Woman
Nice versus Mean
Respecting versus Manipulating
Freedom versus Oppression
Planning versus Impulsiveness
Acceptance versus Rejection
Approval versus Criticism
Harsh versus Soft

Power Dilemmas (25):

Right versus Wrong
Strong versus Weak
Dominant versus Submissive
Manipulator versus Manipulated
Friend versus Enemy
Win versus Lose
Control versus Surrender
Acceptance versus Rejection
Approval versus Criticism
Informed versus Unaware
Better Than versus Less Than
Savvy versus Ignorant
Sophisticated versus Simple
Masculine versus Feminine
One Up versus One Down
Helping versus Hurting
Imagined versus Real
Reputation versus Character
Privilege versus Sweat Equity
Achievement versus Failure
Doing versus Having
Creating versus Destroying
Chaos versus Order

Rich versus Poor
Superior versus Inferior

Success Dilemmas (21):

Gain versus Loss
Win versus Lose
Success versus Failure
Wealth versus Poverty
Affluence versus Lack
Disposable Income versus Debt
Competition versus Cooperation
Individual versus Team
Analysis versus Intuition
Work versus Play
Boss versus Employee
Courage versus Cowardice
Acceptance versus Rejection
Recognition versus Anonymity
Praise versus Blame
Respecting Limits versus Pushing Limits
Expert versus Novice
Problem versus Solution
Planning versus Trial and Error
Perfect versus Mistake
Triumph versus Defeat

Happiness Dilemmas: (26)

Pleasure versus Pain
Gain versus Loss
Holding On versus Letting Go
Being versus Doing
Trust versus Doubt
Positive versus Negative
Blessed versus Cursed

Awake versus Asleep
Conscious versus Unconscious
Relevant versus Useless
Strong versus Weak
Courage versus Cowardice
Clarity versus Confusion
Order versus Chaos
Inner World versus Outer World
Isolated versus Social
Getting What You Want versus Getting What You Don't Want
You versus Me
Health versus Disease
Gratitude versus Grievance
Single versus Paired
Joy versus Sorrow
Full versus Empty
Satisfied versus Frustrated
Serenity versus Discontent
Calm versus Restless

Purpose Dilemmas (21):

Useful versus Useless
Fulfilled versus Longing
Guided versus Lost
Clarity versus Confusion
My Purpose versus Your Purpose
Service versus Servitude
Relevant versus Extraneous
Making Things Happen versus Letting Things Happen
A Part of the Whole versus Separate from the Whole
Rational versus Intuitive
Knowledge versus Ignorance
Safe versus Risky
Commitment versus Indifference
Thinking versus Feeling

Motivated versus Apathetic
Special versus Ordinary
Unique versus Mundane
My Values versus Your Values
Focused versus Scattered
Trust versus Doubt
Real versus Imagined

Faith Dilemmas (31):

Trust versus Doubt
Blind Faith versus Cynicism
Selfish versus Selfless
Truth versus Lie
My Will versus Thy Will
Right versus Wrong
Sin versus Salvation
Sacred versus Profane
Good versus Evil
God versus the Devil
Positive versus Negative
Special versus Ordinary
Heaven versus Hell
Compassion versus Anger
Forgiveness versus Vengeance
Ethical versus Corrupt
Agony versus Ecstasy
Freedom versus Imprisonment
Pride versus Humility
Self-Love versus Self-Hate
Kind versus Mean
Getting Along versus Fighting
Guilt versus Innocence
Control versus Surrender
Acceptance versus Rejection
Angels versus Demons

Wisdom versus Ignorance
Death versus Life
Light versus Darkness
Masculine versus Feminine[13]
Self versus No-Self

WHAT TO DO WITH A LINGERING EMOTIONAL CHARGE

Occasionally there can be a lingering emotional charge still strong enough to create interference. This can result from additional Unresolvable Dilemmas at play in your scenario, or from unresolved distress from past events. (This past may include not only personal history, but also past lives, if you believe in them, and/or ancestral patterns living on in you.)

If this occurs, there are three additional tools you can use: Two are from the world of energy psychology, a method for clearing stuck energy, which we'll explore more in a moment. The other tool is in Step Six: Enjoying the Ride.

You can use these supplementary tools to reduce any remaining emotional charge. Even though you may still feel the emotion in your body, and it may still be uncomfortable, the key is that it no longer feels like a problem. However, you can continue to use these tools until you can no longer find the negative emotion at all around that particular dilemma. Anytime you reduce a heightened emotional charge, you free even more energy for being in the flow of life.

The Magic of Energy Psychology Tools

Energy psychology assumes our brain and body generate, and operate within, an electromagnetic field.[14] This field carries data—sort of like a computer hard drive—and can encounter some glitches that cause the life energy to get stuck. This can make you feel emotionally constipated. Emotional reactions get stuck, and can't move on through.

The tools of energy psychology act like a Roto-Rooter man. They go in and clean out the energy meridians, or channels, where the life energy is blocked, jammed up, or congested due to this heightened emotional charge.

Here are two easy-to-use energy psychology tools you can work with:

Stress Release

You probably already use the Stress Release tool without realizing it.

1. Just place your hand over your forehead and hold it there.

2. Notice where you feel the lingering negative emotion in your body and focus your attention on that spot.

3. Then purposefully wallow in your unwanted feeling or negative belief. Don't try to talk yourself out of it or think positively. Just relax into it and heighten the negative experience by continuing the negative internal dialogue and running the unpleasant scenario.

Your hand on your forehead creates a kind of short-circuit in the way the brain currently codes this reaction. After a bit, the negative emotional charge begins decreasing. How do you know? The intensity you felt in your body has decreased even when you focus on the same negative dialogue and pictures. When you can no longer feel the negative feeling, you know it's worked!

Frontal-Occipital Holding

This tool is exactly like Stress Release with one addition.

1. Again place the palm of one hand over your forehead.

2. Then place the palm of your other hand over the base of your skull, just above the neck.

3. Do exactly what I described for Stress Release above. After a bit, the lingering emotional charge will again be hard to find.

You can find many more energy psychology tools online. Two of the most effective and easy to use are TAT (Tapas Acupressure

Technique—*www.tatlife.com*) and EFT (Emotional Freedom Technique—*www.emofree.com*).

INCREASING YOUR AWARENESS OF OPPOSITES

Learning to think in opposites is powerful. Simple practice develops this skill. Then your unconscious mind will take it over and start giving you the opposite of things as you hear them and think them. You think *me*, it says *you*. You hear *right*, it says *wrong*. You read *acceptance*, it says *rejection*.

Imagine you're preparing for the Polar Pair Olympics. Here are some ways to practice:

- Listen to other people's language and identify the opposites that are not spoken but are operating *unconsciously*: open (closed), fair (unjust), light (dark), kind (cruel), love (hate), close (distant), alone (together), clear (confused), intelligent (stupid), beautiful (ugly), and so on.

- Listen to your own language and identify the opposite that you're not focusing on, which is operating unconsciously for the situation you're describing to make sense: strong (weak), safe (dangerous), love (hate), ally (enemy), pure (tainted), right (wrong), connected (separate), useless (purposeful), happy (sad), energized (depleted), and so on.

- Read a page in the newspaper or a magazine and note the opposite of each word that has an opposing position: liberal (conservative), left (right), famous (anonymous), global (local), rich (poor), security (risk), save (spend), and so on.

- Listen for the unspoken opposites on Sunday morning TV, news programs, and in documentaries.

- While walking to your car, listening to your radio or CDs, or eating out for lunch or dinner, pay attention to what you're hearing and what you're reading on the menus. Look for opposites.

- Focus on opposites for a week—or a full day—or even just an hour a day—and soon you'll be seeing and hearing polar pairs everywhere.

Finding Your Polar Pair via Your Emotions

If all you know for sure is what you're feeling:

1. Name the context or situation where your feeling is happening.

2. In that context, where might the emotion (or experience) be coming from?

3. If it's part of the core polar pair, what would its opposite be?

4. If it's a landmark (strength or weakness) on another polar pair, what polarity could generate the experience?

Example 1: Jane was feeling confused (experience). She wanted to understand her brother (context). In that situation, she felt her confusion was actually one side of the core polar pair—the opposite pole being clarity. They were the two sides of the coin of understanding.

Example 2: Mark was feeling anxious (emotion). He wanted his parents' approval (context). In that situation, he felt anxiety was actually a landmark (a weakness). He named its opposite calm (a strength). The polar pair he thought might be generating these was acceptance and rejection—the two sides of the coin of approval.

FEATURED QUOTES
FROM THE MYSTICS

Intellect divides opposites and makes walls.
Intelligence penetrates opposites and creates bridges.[15]

—OSHO

To set up what you like against what you dislike is the
dis-ease of the mind.
When the deep meaning of things is not understood, the mind's
essential peace is disturbed to no avail.[16]

—SENGSTEN (SOSAN ZENJI)

Love tells me I am everything. Wisdom tells me I am nothing.
Between these two, my life flows.[17]

—SRI NISARGADATTA

Life is not made of contradictions.
It is made of complementary opposites.[18]

—OSHO

The only thing permanent is impermanence.

—HERACLITUS

You cannot step in the same river twice,
for other waters are continually flowing in.

—Heraclitus

Real harmony is neither to go with nor to go against.
Instead, let reality possess you.[19]

—Ta Hui

Allow that which is inescapable to overwhelm you, and you will find
immense peace.[20]

—Ta Hui

Out beyond our ideas of wrongdoing and rightdoing, there is a field.
I'll meet you there.
When the soul lies down in that grass, the world is too full
to talk about.
Ideas, language, even the phrase "each other," doesn't make sense.[21]

—Rumi

NOTES

1. According to Webster's Dictionary, "facticity" refers to the quality of being a fact. I use it to refer to anything that is undeniable, unalterable, and universally verifiable, living in the realm of time and space (that's our world including the realm of the mind or conceptual reality).

2. On the website *HowStuffWorks.com*, William Harris and Robert Lamb describe how invisibility cloaks work. Scientists at the University of Tokyo have developed optical camouflage technology. The results aren't great yet, but scientists were still able to see through objects somewhat. There is also something called "metamaterials," which Harris and Lamb describe as "tiny structures smaller than the wavelength of light. If [a tiny cloak] were properly constructed, it would actually guide rays of invisible light around an object—much like a rock diverting water in a stream." For more information on invisibility cloaks, see the article "How Invisibility Cloaks Work" here: *www.howstuffworks.com/invisibility-cloak.htm*.

3. For more information on the integration of mindfulness meditation and brain research, I recommend Dr. Daniel J. Siegel's book *The Mindful Brain: Reflection and Attunement in the Cultivation of Well-Being*. (New York: W. W. Norton, 2007).

4. For a more in-depth discussion of the Direction Filter, see my first book, *Facticity: a door to mental health and beyond* (Facticity Trainings, Inc., 1991). The Direction Filter is one of what are called "metaprograms" in NLP.

5. Once you understand how to move beyond either/or thinking, the Six-Step Process helps to install new neural pathways into your

actual brain (neurophysiology). I refer to this as upgrading the operating system (your brain) so it can read the new program on opposites and how to handle them. Although I'm not aware of any studies done on the neurological effects of paradoxical thinking per se, I'm hoping some will emerge in the future. The fact remains that after using the process over a period of time, the ability to perceive and effectively manage paradox does emerge.

6. Evidence for this is the emergence of the desired new behavior (using your mystic's eye) without making any conscious effort. The new way of perceiving simply starts happening. For this to occur there has to be a neurological coding for it in the brain since no behavior in the body-mind can occur without it.

7. Neuroplasticity (also referred to as brain plasticity, cortical plasticity, or cortical remapping) is described as "the brain's ability to act and react in ever-changing ways ... This special characteristic allows the brain's estimated 100 billion nerve cells, also called neurons (a.k.a. "gray matter") to constantly lay down new pathways for neural communication and to rearrange existing ones throughout life, thereby aiding the processes of learning, memory, and adaptation through experience. Without the ability to make such functional changes, our brains would not be able to memorize a new fact or master a new skill, form a new memory or adjust to a new environment; we, as individuals, would not be able to recover from brain injuries or overcome cognitive disabilities. Because of the brain's neuroplasticity, old dogs, so to speak, regularly learn new tricks of every conceivable kind." *MemoryZine*, "Introduction to Neuroplasticity," (July 2, 2010). *www.memoryzine.com/2010/07/02/ introduction-to-neuroplasticity.*

8. Living systems theory is a general theory created by James Grier Miller about the existence of all living systems and their structure, interaction, behavior, and development. Living systems according to Parent (International Society for the Systems Sciences, 1996) are by definition "open self-organizing systems that have the special characteristics of life and interact with their environment. This takes place by means of information and material-energy exchanges. Living systems can be as simple as a single cell or as complex as a supranational organization ... Regardless of their

complexity, they each depend upon the same essential twenty subsystems (or processes) in order to survive and to continue the propagation of their species or types beyond a single generation." Elaine Parent, "The Living Systems Theory of James Grier Miller," The Primer Project (n.d.), *www.newciv.org/ISSS_Primer/asem14ep.html.*

9. Noosphere refers to "the sphere of human consciousness and mental activity—especially in regard to its influence on the biosphere and in relation to evolution." Merriam Webster, Incorporated, "Noosphere," Merriam Webster Online (2011).

10. See M. Mitchell Waldrop, *Complexity: The Energy Science at the Edge of Order & Chaos* (New York: Simon & Schuster, 1993) or Melanie Mitchell, *Complexity: A Guided Tour* (New York: Oxford University Press, 2011).

11. This is a biologically driven instinct to move toward pleasure and to move away from pain. That's why I call it hardwired into the brain. You can't delete it or change it. But you can trick it a bit, and that is what you learn in this book—the mystic's trick that harnesses the power of this instinctual drive so it supports your personal transformation rather than hindering it.

12. Research at NASA shows that long-distant views—even just in photographs and posters—induce a sense of "cognitive tranquility," a natural calming of the mind. The calming effect is especially important to maintain performance in high-stress environments. Judith Heerwagen, PhD, and Betty Hase, IIDA, ASID. "Building Biophilia: Connecting People to Nature in Building Design." U.S. Green Building Council (March 8, 2001). *www.usgbc.org/ShowFile.aspx?DocumentID=8543.* Similarly, being distant from your mind-body gives you a new perspective on it—and although the distance may not be measured in miles, the effect is as life-changing as seeing the Earth from afar was on the astronauts' perspective. Based on this experience, Edgar Mitchell founded IONS, an organization dedicated to finding ways to replicate the experience he had when traveling back from the moon, ways to explore shifting consciousness itself. (*www.noetic.org*)

13. People's faith seems to be tied up in either a masculine view of God/Higher Self, etc. or a feminine view, and they each have differing characteristics—i.e., challenge/rightness/power usually refers to male, and acceptance/love/compassion usually refers to female. People polarize to these and argue over the male or female nature of the Universe or God.

14. Fred Gallo, PhD, states: "Energy psychology addresses the relationship of energy systems to emotion, cognition, behavior, and health. These systems include electrical activity of the nervous system and heart, meridians, biophotons, biofields, etc. Although psychological functioning involves thought, emotions, chemistry, neurology, genetics and environmental aspects, at an essential level bioenergy is also involved. . . . Energy psychology is applicable to a wide range of areas including psychotherapy, counseling, education, vocational guidance, physical health, pain management, sports and peak performance." "What is Energy Psychology?" Energy Psychology (n.d.), *www.energypsych.com/what-is-energy-psychology/*. Energy Psychology is a registered trademark by Fred P. Gallo, PhD, and VAK Verlags GmbH.

15. Osho, *Om Shantih Shantih Shantih: The Soundless Sound, Peace Peace Peace* (New York: Osho International Foundation, 1988), chapter 5, "Love Gives Your Legs a Dance."

16. Seng-ts'an, *The Hsin Hsin Ming: Verses on the Faith-Mind*, trans. Dr. Richard B. Clarke (Louisville: White Pines Press, 2001). Originally published in 1975 in Poona by the Rajneesh Foundation. This was the subject of Rajneesh discourses given in October 1974.

17. Osho, *Om Shantih Shantih Shantih*, chapter 5.

18. *Ibid.*

19. Ta Hui, *Swampland Flowers: The Letters and Lectures of Zen Master Ta Hui*, trans. J.C. Cleary (Boston: Shambhala Publications, Inc., 2006).

20. *Ibid.*

21. Rumi, *The Essential Rumi,* trans. Coleman Barks with John Moyne (San Francisco: HarperSanFrancisco, 1995) 36.